Teaching Strings

Teaching Strings

Technique and Pedagogy

Robert H. Klotman

Schirmer Books
A Division of Macmillan, Inc.
New York
Collier Macmillan Publishers
London

Schirmer Books
A Division of Macmillan, Inc.
866 Third Avenue, New York, NY 10022

Collier Macmillan Canada, Inc.

Library of Congress Catalog Card No.: 87-22880

Printed in the United States of America

printing number
1   2   3   4   5   6   7   8   9   10

Library of Congress Cataloging-in-Publication Data

Klotman, Robert H.
    Teaching strings / Robert H. Klotman.
    p. cm.
    Bibliography: p.
    ISBN 0-02-870961-6
    1. Stringed instruments, Bowed—Instruction and study. I. Title.
MT259.K58 1988
787'.01'0712—dc19   87-22880
                                                         CIP
                                                         MN

    Excerpts from Phyllis Young, *Playing the String Games: Strategies for
Teaching Cello and Strings*, © 1978 by the University of Texas Press,
have been reprinted here by permission of the publisher and the author.

    The example of scordatura tuning from Richard Felciano, "O He Did Whistle
and She Did Sing," © 1972 by E. C. Shirmer Music Co., Inc., Boston,
has been reprinted here by permission of the publisher.

Dedicated to the memory of ERNEST E. HARRIS,
adviser, colleague, collaborator, and friend.

Contents

Songs and Literature

Preface

The preparation of string teachers has an interesting past. There have been several approaches in general practice. The early, so-called methods courses for the preparation of teachers of instrumental music placed stress on the lecture system. The expectation was that the college teacher would explain the principles and practices, and the student would read about the subject and possibly observe some actual teaching situations where these methods were applied in the classroom.

Another prevalent view is that the best preparation for teachers of instruments or groups of instruments lies in the acquisition of as much skill as possible in the actual playing of the instrument. The theory here is simply that one should be able to do what one is attempting to teach others to do. In this approach the usual pattern is to teach the future teacher actually to play the instrument involved, using the same material that the young students will use. Certainly one of the strongest objections to this idea is that the college-level student, a somewhat mature adult, has been forced to spend too much time with musical literature at a far more immature level than is justified.

In recent years educators have come to recognize that students in higher education should have material especially designed for their level of musical maturity, even as they are acquiring knowledge about elementary instrumental performance. Most of the publications thus far either have emphasized the verbalization of method—in which case there is insufficient musical material for full realization of the principle involved—or else have consisted primarily of music to be played, without sufficient explanation of concepts, principles, and practices. This textbook integrates the musical material with a minimum but essential verbalization.

The text seeks to provide a broad view of the total string-instruction program in a well-planned sequence for the training of the future string teacher. It includes references to the preschool child, as exemplified in the Suzuki approach, action and body-motion studies, as advocated by Paul Rolland, and rote-to-note practices. Orchestras are constantly confronted with a shortage of string players. They look to the schools for assistance. It is our contention that the student who goes through school having a vital experience in string performance will be more likely, as an adult, to contribute to the arts either as a performer or as a supporter.

To assist the student in progressing through the text, competencies in the form of clearly stated objectives are provided. These competencies were selected through analyzing the necessary skills a beginning teacher needs to organize and teach young string classes. They are arranged in a sequence so that when a student acquires each one as he or she moves to the next competency, he or she will develop the skills essential for teaching strings.

Another feature of this book is the built-in provision for student self-evaluation. It identifies activities designed to develop each competency and students may self-check their progress as they proceed from one competency to another. Incidentally, the answer for each self-evaluation question should be YES, unless otherwise indicated, and students should make adjustments to arrive at the YES answer as they progress.

Acknowledgments

The author wishes to express gratitude and appreciation to the following contributors who have allowed use of their materials:

Edward Campbell, luthier, The Chimneys Violin Shop
Walter Coplin, string bass teacher, West Virginia University
Peter Horn, Horn and Son Stringed Instruments
Heinrich Roth, past president of Scherl and Roth Company
Kent Miller, Photographer, Indiana University Audio-Visual Center

and to the following individuals who posed for the illustrations:

Stella Anderson, viola/violin instructor, MacPhail Center for the Arts, Minneapolis
Cory Cerovsek, violin student, Indiana University
Darin Chertkoff, cellist, College for Gifted and Talented Youth, Indiana University
Simone Gubar, cellist, College for Gifted and Talented Youth, Indiana University
William Koehler, string bass, professor, Illinois State University

Part I
General Information
Regarding String Instruments

Construction and Nomenclature

Competency 1:	Be able to name the various parts of the body of the string instruments, back and front.
Competency 1.1:	Be able to name the various parts of the bow.

Construction of String Instruments

The best string instruments are made from wood. In the interest of budgets that affect school economy and the grueling use that many instruments receive, some acceptable substitute materials have been developed. Under no circumstances, however, should substitutes be used if they distort tonal images and basic sound.

The tops of string instruments are usually made of even, narrow-grained spruce. The head, the neck, the sides or ribs, and the bridge are made of various grades of maple. The nut, the fingerboard, the saddle, and the inlaid purfling should be made of ebony. The pegs, tail-piece, and end button are usually ebony but they may also be rosewood or boxwood.

Chin rests will vary. They may be made of ebony, rosewood, boxwood, or a plastic. The best end pins are made of steel and should be adjustable. The string bass has mechanical, geared pegs. These should be mounted on a brass plate.

One of the acceptable substitutes may be laminated wood, sometimes used for the top, back, and sides of cellos or basses; it should be carefully checked for quality. Fiberglass basses have been found to be most economical and quite satisfactory for school use.

The finish should be of high-quality, polished varnish. Lacquer is not acceptable for string instruments.

Bows

The better bows are made of Pernambuco wood. A good quality brazilwood may be an adequate substitute, but under no circumstances should one accept beechwood. Fiberglass bows have proved extremely satisfactory for school use.

Nomenclature of String Instruments

All string instruments use the same nomenclature for the various parts. Since the cello and bass rest on the floor, they have additional items such as an end pin and an adjusting screw that keeps the end pin in place. (Naturally there is no chin rest on the cello or bass.)

It is important that the string teacher be able to identify the parts by their correct terms, since these are the common language of string players. In addition, using the correct terms prevents misunderstanding when having repairs made by mail or phone. As obvious as this advice seems, there is a disconcerting amount of confusion created because the simple knowledge of terms is not applied.

Figure 1-1

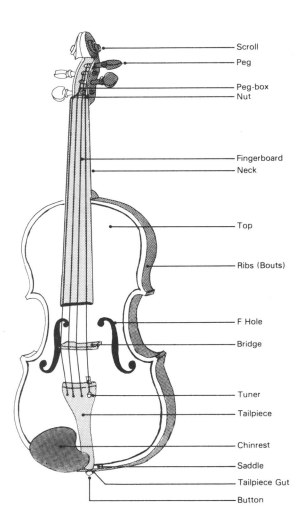

Scroll
Peg
Peg-box
Nut

Fingerboard
Neck

Top

Ribs (Bouts)

F Hole

Bridge

Tuner
Tailpiece

Chinrest
Saddle
Tailpiece Gut
Button

Figure 1-1 shows a front exterior view of the parts of a violin or viola; Figure 1-2 shows the rear exterior of a string bass. (When comparing a violin and viola, note that the viola is slightly larger in all dimensions.) Figure 1-3 shows a cross section of the interior.

Figure 1-2

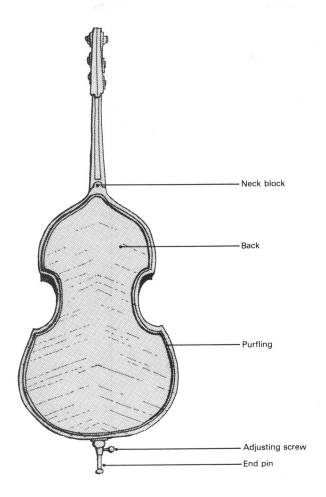

- Neck block
- Back
- Purfling
- Adjusting screw
- End pin

Figure 1-3

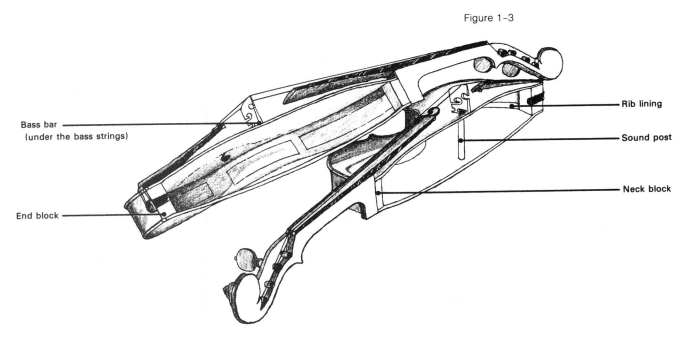

- Rib lining
- Sound post
- Neck block

Bass bar
(under the bass strings)

End block

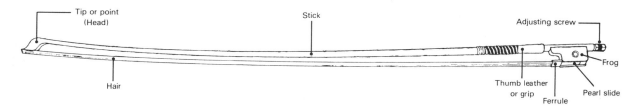

Tip or point
(Head)

Stick

Adjusting screw

Hair

Thumb leather
or grip

Frog

Ferrule

Pearl slide

Figure 1–4

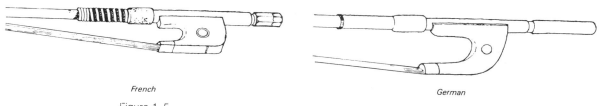

French

German

Figure 1–5

The Bow

The nomenclature for the bow is the same for each instrument (see Fig. 1–4). The bows of the different instruments vary in size and thickness of each part in proportion to the stick.

The only instrument with two styles of bow is the string bass, which may be played with either a French or German ("Butler") style bow (see Fig. 1–5). However, the French conforms to the bows of the other members of the string family and is the more popular in string classes.

Activities and Check List

1. Select a string instrument and name each part as you point to it.
2. Select a violin, viola, or violoncello bow and name each part as you point to it.
3. Describe the different distinguishing features of the French- and German-style bass bows. Indicate by pointing to the different parts.
4. Indicate the distinguishing features among the violin, viola, and violoncello bows (length and thickness).
5. Describe the materials that are used in the construction of string instruments and their various accessories. (See pp. 3, 8, and 9.)

Care and Maintenance of String Instruments

> Competency 2: Be able to identify the rules for care and repair that apply to all string instruments.

A careful program of preventive maintenance can save a great deal of money and time; it can also prevent unnecessary damage and abuses that lead to costly repairs.

A few simple rules that apply to all string instruments are as follows:

1. After each playing, use a soft cloth to remove all rosin dust from the instrument and from all parts of the bow except, of course, the hair itself.
2. Always keep the instrument and bow in the case when not in use.
3. Be certain that the latches on the case are always closed.
4. Loosen the bow hair enough so that the tension is removed from the arch of the stick when the bow is not in use. Three complete turns of the adjusting screw is usually sufficient. A corollary to this principle is to avoid excessive tension in the stick when tightening the bow. It should never be so tight that the arch is removed.
5. The bridge should be tilted slightly back toward the tailpiece.
6. String adjustors should not be turned all the way down so that they scratch the top of the instrument.
7. Do not permit students to stuff music into their instrument cases.
8. If pegs are slipping, they may be treated with a commercial "peg dope." However, this is only a temporary solution and the pegs should be eventually replaced or refitted.
9. Worn gears on string basses, adjustment screws on tuners, and adjustment screws on the cell or bass end pins may all be lubricated with vaseline, used sparingly.
10. Improperly fitted pegs should be adjusted only by a competent repairman or shop.

The bridge is kept in position by the pressure of the strings. Under *no* circumstances should it be glued to the top. (In fact, nothing should be glued except by an expert.) The *high* side of the bridge is under the following strings for the various instruments: G string on the violin, C string on the viola, C string on the cello, and E string on the string bass.

A great deal of unnecessary repair work results from improper storage. Keep instruments out of excessively dry areas or damp basements and away from radiators and hot air registers. An ideal temperature is about 60 degrees Fahrenheit with a relative humidity of about 45–50%. Loosen the strings when storing for an extended period of time.

Be certain that storage facilities are constructed in such a manner that the instruments cannot fall or bump each other. The cost of proper construction for storage is a saving well worth the investment.

Competency 3:	Be able to identify the essentials for proper adjustment of string instruments.

Purchasing String Equipment

When selecting string instruments for school or private use, the manner of construction and the materials used, as described in the preceding sections, should be carefully noted. "Playability" of string instruments is so dependent on proper construction and correct adjustment and alignment that it is recommended that instruments conform to these standards regardless of the price bracket in which they may fall. The selection of instruments should not be based solely on a low initial price. So often inferior instruments eventually cost more than better ones in terms of repairs and loss of instruction time. The table on page 233 lists standard and junior sizes of string instruments.

A few comments on specifications are in order.

1. All string instruments should be hand made and individually planed, sandpapered, adjusted, and tested.
2. Instruments should be made of matched woods that have been seasoned for a minimum of seven years.
3. Construction:
   a. All joints should be glued tightly and reinforced with four full corner blocks and solid upper and lower blocks, and with full lining inside of top and back.
   b. All edges should be glued securely.
   c. Cracks, if any, should be properly repaired (reinforced and glued).
   d. Inlaid purfling is preferred.
   e. Bass bar should be of harder spruce than wood used for top itself. Bass bar must be glued in and not carved out from top wood.
4. Trimmings:
   a. Pegs—ebony or rosewood. Pegs such as "nonslip" by Caspari or DeJacques are recommended.
   b. Fingerboard—ebony. For basses and cellos it may be of rosewood treated to resist absorption.
   c. Nut and saddle—ebony.
   d. Tailpiece—ebony.

5. Attachments
    a. Chin rests—ebony, plastic, or rosewood.
    b. Strings—good quality, properly matched.
        E (violin): stainless steel with adjuster
        A (violin, viola, violoncello): gut or aluminum wound on gut
        D (all instruments): aluminum wound on gut
        G (all instruments): silver wound on gut
        C (viola, cello): silver wound on gut
        String-bass strings are primarily made of steel. Steel strings always should be provided with adjusters (violin, viola, cello).

Proper Adjustment

One of the hidden costs in the procurement and maintenance of string instruments is the expense involved in proper adjustment. One cannot place enough emphasis on this item. It is of utmost importance since it affects intonation, tone quality, ease of playing, and basic instruction. A less expensive instrument with the proper adjustment is far more valuable for a student's development than a fine, expensive instrument improperly adjusted.

Imported instruments are packed in cases, shipped across oceans, and stored for extended periods of time to await delivery. The extreme humidity encountered during the voyage and the sharp climatic changes will cause changes in the various wood parts of the instruments. This problem alone contributes much to the maladjustment of the string equipment.

Some of the items to examine for proper adjustment are the following:

1. *Peg alignment.* Pegs should be properly fitted so that they are snug at both sides of the peg box. In addition, they should be aligned in such a way that there is adequate clearance for each string above the peg in front of it. Under no circumstances should the end of the string be in a position where it can be forced into the peg-box wall.

2. *Fingerboard.* The fingerboard should be slightly concave without any warpage. When warped or worn, it interferes with intonation and causes a buzzing sound. A simple ruler placed on edge on top of the fingerboard will quickly indicate any warping.

3. *Fingerboard nut.* The nut should be checked carefully to see that it is not too low and that the spacing of the string grooves is correct so that the strings may enter the peg box and be wound properly.

4. *Bridge.* The entire surface of each foot of the bridge should be in contact with the top of the instrument. The height must be correct so that it does not require excessive finger pressure to play. If it is too low, it will interfere with the tone and hinder proper finger placement. The grooves should be deep enough to hold each string in place.

5. *Tailpiece.* The end of the tailpiece should come even with the center of the saddle but not extend beyond it. Under no circumstances should the tailpiece touch the body of the instrument or any of its components (chin rest, etc.).

6. *End pin.* On the cello and the bass be certain that the end pin slides freely and can be easily adjusted to the height of the player.

7. *Sound post.* The sound post is located immediately behind the right foot of the bridge. The distance between the back of the bridge and the front of the post is approximately one-half of the thickness of the post.

8. *Bow.* The bow wire should be silver and soldered at each end. The bow screen should turn freely and the frog should be seated securely so that it does not wobble. Check to see that the hair tightens evenly to a desirable amount of tension and, conversely, that it may be properly but not excessively relaxed when the frog is in full forward position. Tighten the stick about two or three turns and sight down it to be certain that it is straight.

9. *Bow Hair.* For a variety of reasons, such as oil from contact with the skin, dust, or just rubbing, the hairs on the bow fail to hold Rosin. When a player "feels" that the hairs are not gripping the string, he should replace them. This may be necessary even while the bow still has its full knot of hair.

10. *Strings.* Ideally, strings are matched for perfect fifths. When a string becomes false, it is virtually impossible to tune and the tone is affected. False strings should be replaced. (Do not wait until they break.) Long before an E string goes false, it becomes "dead." Although it still may be reasonably true in pitch, it no longer has the clear, ringing brilliance it had, especially in the high register. The violin E should be changed frequently. (The single most dramatic thing that can be done to improve the sound of the school's violin section is to have all of the violinists change their E strings a week before a concert or contest.)

Activities and Check List

1. If this course is taught in a class, exchange instruments and examine each one to see how good proper care and maintenance are.
2. Recommend needed repairs and replacement of parts for the instruments examined.

Selecting the Proper-Sized Instrument

It is essential that students be given instruments in direct proportion to their growth. Nothing is more discouraging to the beginner than to be forced to play with the handicap of learning on an instrument that is too small or too large for his or her physical stature (see Fig. 2–1). Because sizes vary dramatically within age

Figure 2-1

groups, it is difficult to set up a definite structure for selecting instrument size. Each individual must be measured in accordance with his or her physical development (see Fig. 2–2).

Figure 2-2

Violin and viola. Extend the student's left arm palm up, and select the size instrument that enables him or her to curl fingers around the scroll and into the peg box comfortably.

Cello. When holding the instrument with the knees, at the bouts, it should allow the student to have correct left-hand position. If the position is correct, the student should be able to play a minor third between the first and fourth finger without distorting the fingers (see pp. 20 and 63).

Double bass.   The height of the instrument should be so that the nut is approximately at level with the student's eyes and he or she should be able to play a major second comfortably between the first and fourth fingers (see pp. 23 and 64). Note that the size should also be determined by the length of the student's bow arm when placing the bow at the middle on the D string. The shoulders should remain fairly horizontal.

Activities and Check List

1. Examine your instrument and bow and see if it complies with the adjustments you identified.
2. Exchange instruments and bows with others in the class and check their equipment for adjustment.
3. Make a list of adjustments that need to be made on any of the above, if any are needed, and submit it for shop correction.

Part II
Early Instruction

Holding the Instruments

Competency 4:	Be able to specify and identify correct left-hand position for holding your instrument.

Holding the Instruments

Violin and Viola

To acquire the proper playing position the student should proceed through the following steps.

1. With the strings of the instrument facing away from the body, place the left hand on the right bout of the violin and the right hand on the bout where the chin rest is located (see Fig. 3–1).

Figure 3–1

15

2. Swing the instrument into place on the left collar-bone with the button holding the tailpiece gut aimed at the "Adam's apple" (Fig. 3-2).

Figure 3-2

3. Turn the head to the left so that the jaw may drop comfortably into the chin rest. Get a sufficiently secure grip so that the left hand may be removed and the instrument still will be retained by the grip between the jaw and the collarbone (Fig. 3-3). To get the feel of this grip, it is sometimes advisable to substitute the fingers of the right hand for the jaw and press on the chin rest so that the student feels the support between the fingers and the collarbone.

Figure 3-3

4. Sight down the fingerboard and note that the scroll should be at the level of the tip of the nose. Whether sitting or standing, the student should be certain that his or her back is straight and his or her weight evenly distributed so that there is good balance at all times.

Left-hand position.   During open-string rote exercises (see Fig. 3–3), it is advisable to keep the palm of the left hand on the right bout. However, once the fingers of the left hand are brought into use, the proper left-hand position should be established.

1. With the instrument held securely by the jaw and collarbone, move the entire hand back to the nut at the end of the fingerboard.

2. The neck of the instrument should be approximately at the first joint from the *tip* of the thumb. (This will vary according to the size of the thumb and fingers.) The base joint of the first finger should be level with the top of the fingerboard.

3. The thumb should be opposite the first finger or between the first and second fingers, as shown in Figure 3–4 (Some prefer it slightly behind or slightly in front. This will depend on the length of the fingers.) Of utmost importance is that the thumb and first finger form an open "C" so that the hand is free to move up and down the neck. The heel or palm should *not* touch the under part of the neck (see "Common Errors in Posture").

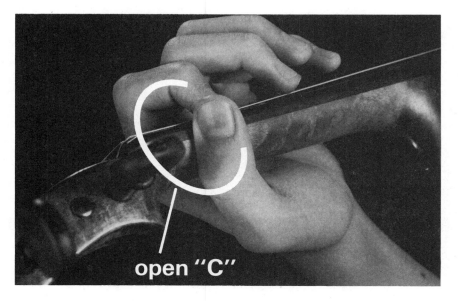

Figure 3-4

open "C"

4. The left elbow joint should be under the center of the violin. This will vary according to the string that is being played on and the length of the student's left arm. (It is desirable that the left elbow be pointed more to the right than to the left.)

It is not important whether the violinist or violist stand or sit when playing as long as he or she is standing or sitting properly.

When playing in an ensemble, performers are usually seated. In private lessons or in a solo performance standing is preferable.

Standing position.   Most important is the position of the feet. They should be about 10 to 12 inches apart with the left foot slightly in front of the right or the feet should be in line with each other. Basically, the body's weight should be balanced and equally distributed on both feet so that performers can shift their weight comfortably in either direction. Above all, students should avoid a rigid posture; they should be capable of moving in a flexible, flowing manner in whatever direction assists in proper bowing. (See Fig. 3–5.)

Figure 3–5

Sitting position.   When performing in a sitting position, the violinist or violist should sit on the edge of the chair with both feet on the floor. To avoid having the right knee interfere with the bow he or she should move the right foot slightly back, raising the heel, thus lowering the right knee cap. Under no circumstances should performers be permitted to play with their legs crossed. It

Figure 3-6

interferes with proper bow movement and body balance. (See Fig. 3-6.)

Violoncello

To acquire the proper playing position for the cello, proceed in the following sequence:

1. Select a chair with a straight, level seat that will permit the performer to lean forward slightly. Avoid chairs that slope backward, for example, folding chairs.

2. Adjust the end pin so that when the instrument is placed between the knees, the upper rim of the cello at the neck block rests against the player's chest, just where the bones of the rib cage part (see Figs. 3-7 and 3-8). The corner of the lower bout is in contact with the left knee, while the right knee braces the instrument on the opposite bout as *it is tilted slightly to the right* (see Fig. 3-9). Both feet are generally flat on the floor; however, tall individuals with long legs may choose to bend the right leg behind them.

Figure 3-7

Figure 3-8

Figure 3-9

3. Check that the end pin rests on the floor in a line with the center of the body. The scroll should barely clear the student's left shoulder. It should not rest on his or her shoulder. A good reference point is that the bottom tuning peg is at about the left ear lobe when the head is held erect. (Be careful that the instrument is only an inch or two from the left side of the player's neck.)

Left-hand position.   The fingers of the left hand are virtually at right angles with the strings. They should be arched with the thumb opposite the second finger. The thumb acts as a natural support for the arch of the hand, and its tip should be at about the middle of the neck of the cello. To find this position, use the following sequence:

1. Raise the left arm so that it is parallel to the floor with the palm facing down and the fingers and wrist relaxed.
2. Bend the elbow, bringing the ball of the thumb behind the neck of the instrument and the fingers over the string in an arched position. Roll the thumb slightly on its side opposite the second finger to give support to the hand.
3. Check the following:
    a. The elbow and wrist should be in a *straight* line with the fingers.
    b. The thumb should not grip the neck but should form an open "C" with the second finger (see Fig. 3–10).

Figure 3–10

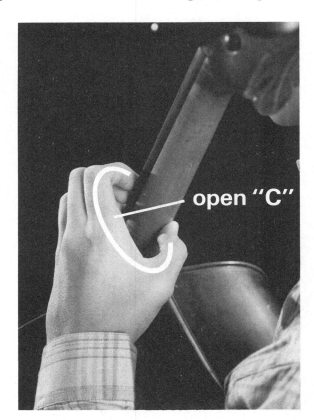

open "C"

c. The fingers should be in an arched position just over the strings, ready to play each note.

d. Since the level of the strings over the fingerboard varies, the left elbow and forearm will change level as the hand moves from string to string (higher for the lower strings). In addition, as the hand moves to the lower strings, the thumb will also move slightly to the left of the neck of the instrument.

String Bass

The performer's body should be against the instrument in a manner that will permit the most durable position for bowing with the right hand, fingering the strings with the left hand. Neither hand should be favored when establishing position. It is of utmost importance that both hands be able to function appropriately without handicaps from inappropriate posture.*

To acquire the proper playing position, follow these steps (see Figs. 3–11, 3–12, and 3–13):

*The angle of the body in relation to the instrument will depend on whether the student is playing a "French" or "German" style bow.

Figure 3-11

Figure 3-12

Figure 3-13

1. Balance the body so that initially the weight is distributed on both feet. Hold the left side of the instrument with the left hand extended straight out in front, and center the instrument in front of the left foot.

2. Turn the bass a quarter turn to the right, and bring it toward the inside of the players left thigh and knee. (The left foot may be placed on a rung of a chair or stool.) At the same time, turn the left foot at an oblique angle and bend the left knee toward the back of the instrument. The back edge of the right bout should rest against the performer's left groin.

3. Note that the bass is brought toward the player so that it leans against him. In this position it is balanced between the knee, the left thigh, and the abdomen, leaving the left hand completely free. The weight should now be shifted to the right foot. (Many professionals use a stool when playing as is shown in Figure 3-14. However, students *should learn to play standing*. Once the proper playing position is well established, they may use a stool in lengthy rehearsals; however, when doing so, they *must* employ the same principles learned when standing). Incidentally, the stool may be useful in teaching vibrato and shifting since it contributes to a more relaxed left hand.

Figure 3-14

4. The nut at the end of the fingerboard should be approximately at the student's eye level and the right arm should be able to reach comfortably the proper bowing position. (This will vary according to the student's height and arm length.)

5. Adjust the end pin on the bass so that it is at the appropriate height for the student. Another aid might be, when the left hand is in half position, it will be approximately opposite the performer's cheek. The right arm should be fully extended when drawing the bow across the strings. It should be straight but not rigid. (See Figs. 3–11 and 3–12.)

Left-hand position. The fingers of the left hand are virtually at right angles with the strings and are slightly arched over the strings in such a way that the fleshy pads of the fingers will fall in place on the strings. The inside corner of the thumb is placed against the neck of the bass opposite the second finger. The left elbow is *slightly* below the hand's level with the first finger acting as an extension of the forearm. (See Fig. 3–15.) The distance between the first and second fingers is the equivalent of one half step, while the space between the second and fourth fingers is an additional half step.

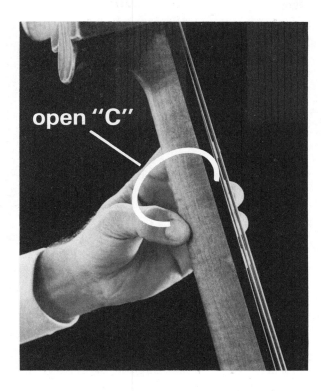

open "C"

Figure 3-15

To acquire the proper posture, proceed as follows:

1. Raise the left arm so that it is parallel to the floor, with the palm of the hand down.
2. Bend the elbow and, without dropping the elbow, turn the hand and bring the ball of the thumb behind the neck of the instrument, with the tip of the thumb at about the middle of the neck of the bass and the fingers above the fingerboard.
3. Roll the thumb so that the ball rests slightly on its side opposite the second finger.
4. Align the fourth finger so that it forms a straight line with the elbow. The first finger is pointed upward so that it appears to be aimed at the nose. The third finger automatically moves down with the fourth finger.

Note that the thumb does not grip the neck but rests on it opposite the second finger, forming an open "C."

Since the level of the strings over the fingerboard varies, the left elbow and forearm will change levels as the hand moves from string to string. The thumb will also move slightly to the left of the neck of the instrument as the fingers move to the lower strings.

Activities for Violin/Viola/Violoncello/Double Bass

1. Observe yourself in a mirror and check to see if you are demonstrating the proper left-hand position on your instrument (violin, viola, cello or double bass).

Self-Check List for Violin/Viola

	Yes	No
a. Is the *jaw* in the chin rest?	☐	☐
b. Are you able to drop your left hand and hold the instrument with jaw and the collarbone?	☐	☐
c. Is the instrument fairly parallel with the floor?	☐	☐
d. Is the left elbow joint under the instrument?	☐	☐
e. Are the left-hand fingers curved over the string so that you would be putting the finger tips down on the string? (See Fig. 3–4.)	☐	☐
f. Is the thumb pointed toward the ceiling opposite the first finger or between the first and second fingers? (See Fig. 3–4.)	☐	☐
g. Do the thumb and first finger form an open "C" so that the neck of the violin is *not* down in the web between the fingers? (See Fig. 3–4.)	☐	☐

Self-Check List for Violoncello

	Yes	No
a. Is the end pin at the proper height so that the neck block rests just where the bones of the rib cage part?	☐	☐
b. Is the end pin resting on the floor in a line with the center of the body?	☐	☐
c. The scroll is *not* resting on your shoulder.	☐	☐
d. When putting the left-hand fingers in playing position are they virtually at right angles with the strings?	☐	☐
e. Are the fingers arched with the thumb opposite the second finger?	☐	☐
f. Are the elbow and wrist in a straight line with the fingers?	☐	☐
g. Does the thumb form and open "C" with the second finger?	☐	☐

Self-Check List for Double Bass

	Yes	No
a. Is the end pin at the proper height so that the nut at the end of the fingerboard is approximately at your eye level?	☐	☐
b. Are you able to balance the bass between your knee, thigh, and abdomen so that your left hand is sufficiently free to remove it from the neck? (Try it!)	☐	☐
c. When placing your fingers in playing position, are they at right angles with the strings?	☐	☐
d. Is the thumb opposite the second finger?	☐	☐
e. Is the fourth finger in a straight line with the elbow?	☐	☐
f. Is the first finger pointed upward?	☐	☐

2. Teach the left-hand position for your instrument to another student who does not play the one you are learning.

Competency 4.1:	Be able to specify and identify correct right-hand position for holding your violin/viola bow, violoncello bow, or double-bass bow.

Holding the Bow

Holding the Violin Bow

Steps for learning proper bow position for violin and viola are as follows:

1. Hold the bow on the screw with the left hand, with the bow hair toward the body (Fig. 3–16).
2. Place the inside tip of the right thumb on the stick against the corner of the frog.
3. Bend the thumb so that the upper part of it touches the hair. Whether or not it touches will vary with teachers, but it is advisable to start with this concept to be sure that the *thumb is bent* (see "Common Errors in Posture").
4. Place the second finger opposite the thumb with the stick crossing the crease in the first joint from the tip of the finger. Let the first finger fall on the stick across the middle joint.
5. Place the third finger comfortably alongside the second finger with its tip pointing toward the pearl inset on the frog.
6. Then place the fourth finger in *an arched position* on top of the inner side of the stick. The fourth finger must be curved. In this position the joints of the fingers are inclined toward the tip of the bow (Figs. 3–17 and 3–18). Be certain that all the fingers are curved and pulled "into the stick."

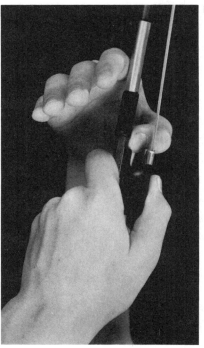

Figure 3–16

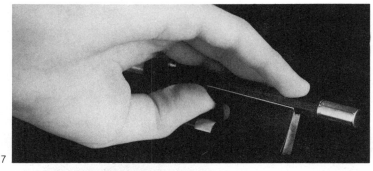

Figure 3–17

Figure 3–18

Figure 3-19

Figure 3-20

When placing the bow in playing position at the frog, the student should tilt the bow slightly with the hair toward the bridge at an angle. As the bow approaches the middle, he should flatten the angle so that from the middle to the point the full hair is used. As he approaches the point, or tip, of the bow he should have the feeling that he is pushing the bow away from him. The process should be reversed when moving from the tip to the frog. Note the angle of the left wrist in Figures 3-19, 3-20, and 3-21. Except in playing the cello (see discussion in the following section), the bow moves parallel to the bridge.

Figure 3-21

For "down-bow" on violins and violas, the left arm forms an imaginary triangle at the frog, a square at the middle of the bow, and then moves away from the body at the point. For the "up-bow," the arm merely traverses the return path, applying the same angles at the middle and frog.

Holding the Cello Bow

To acquire the correct bow position (Figs. 3–22 and 3–23):

1. With the left hand, hold the stick at the middle and parallel to the floor, with the hair facing the floor.
2. Bring the right arm up from the elbow so that the forearm is parallel to the floor, with the left hand hanging down and the fingers and wrist completely relaxed.
3. Place the right side of the thumb on the stick against the corner of the frog and arch the thumb slightly. The middle, or second finger should be opposite the thumb, with the stick resting against the middle joint.
4. Curve the first finger slightly around the bow grip at the middle joint of the finger.
5. Then place the fourth finger approximately at the middle of the frog (where the pearl inset might be) with the first joint curved *over* the stick.
6. The third finger falls naturally in place beside the fourth finger.

All fingers on the bow are rounded and slightly separated. Avoid stiffness and tense, straight lines. The degree to which the fingers will fall in place or be rounded will be determined by the length of the fingers and the size of the hand.

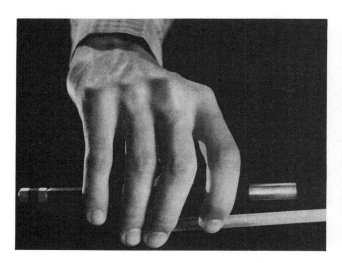

Figure 3-22

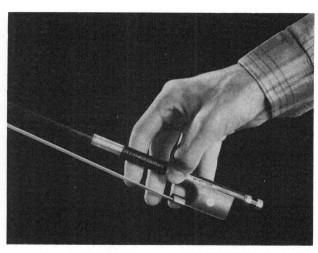

Figure 3-23

The cello bow moves in an arc around the bridge as it moves from string to string (Figs. 3–24, 3–25, and 3–26).

Figure 3-24

Figure 3-25

Figure 3-26

Holding the French Bass Bow

To acquire the correct bow position:

1. With the left hand hold the stick parallel to the floor at the center with the hair facing the floor.
2. Slightly curve the right thumb and place the tip of the right side of it on the stick against the frog (see Fig. 3–27). It should be opposite the second finger, which is in contact with the bow at the second joint from the tip.
3. The first finger falls over the stick and curves slightly over the bow grip at the middle joint.
4. Drop the fourth finger over the frog at the first joint from the tip so that it hangs approximately at the pearl inset of the frog.

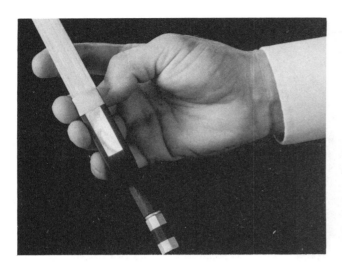

Figure 3-27

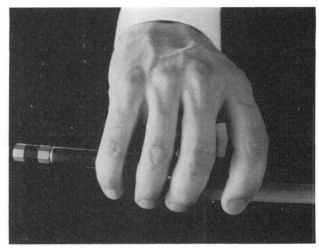

Figure 3-28

5. Allow the third finger to fall in place alongside the second finger (see Fig. 3–28).

The fingers are slightly spread and pulled into the stick. Raymond Benner of the Detroit Symphony suggests that one can accomplish a proper bow "hold" and "feel" if he imagines that the stick is like an archer's bow with the stick being the bowstring. By holding the bow out with your left hand as if you were putting an arrow in it, and then pulling the stick with your right hand as if to shoot an arrow, you will get the proper position and the necessary curve in the right fingers for the "pull" utilized when playing.

Holding the German Bass Bow

1. With the fingers of the right hand extended, place the screw section of the bow into the web between the thumb and the first finger.
2. Bend the thumb so that it lies on top of the stick and is turned slightly outward. Place the fourth finger underneath the frog, providing support for the frog, and allow the first and second fingers, slightly curved, to rest against the side of the bow. The third finger rests in the curve of the frog (Figs. 3–29 and 3–30).

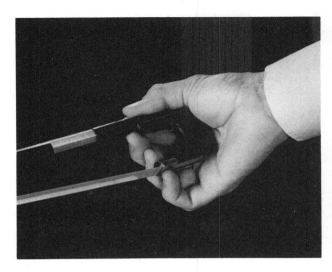

Figure 3-29

Figure 3-30

Activities and Check List for Violin/Viola

1. With the bow in playing position, turn your wrist over so that the bow hair is facing the ceiling and observe the following:

	Yes	No
a. Is the inside tip of the right thumb *on the stick against* the corner of the frog?	☐	☐
b. Is the thumb *bent*?	☐	☐
c. Is the thumb opposite the second finger?	☐	☐
d. Is the fourth finger (little finger) curved and on *top* of the stick?	☐	☐
e. Are the fingers inclined toward the tip of the bow?	☐	☐

Activities and Check List for Violoncello and French Bass Bow

1. With the bow in playing position, look in a mirror and observe the following:

	Yes	No
a. Is the thumb slightly curved and opposite the second finger?	☐	☐
b. Is the fourth finger *over* the frog so that the stick passes through the end joint of the little finger?	☐	☐
c. Are the fingers rounded?	☐	☐
d. When you turn the stick over so that the hair faces the ceiling, is the curved thumb against the corner of the frog?	☐	☐

Activities and Check List for German Bass Bow

1. With the bow in playing position, observe the following: Yes   No
   a. Is the thumb bent slightly and on top of the stick and
      turned slightly outward?   ☐   ☐
   b. Is the fourth finger underneath the frog with the stick
      resting on the fleshy part of the little finger? (See Fig.
      3–29.)   ☐   ☐
2. For all instruments, teach the bow-hand position for your instrument to
   another student who does not play your instrument.

> Competency 4.2:   Be able to recognize common errors in
>   posture visually.

Common Errors in Posture: Visual Clues

In teaching string instruments, it is essential to be able to observe
errors by sight as well as sound. Careful observation may prevent
poor playing habits and difficulties that might occur as the student
progresses. The illustrations shown in Figures 3–31 through 47 are
visual clues to improper body balance that causes tension, fatigue,
and poor performance. Proper playing positions are shown on pages
17–33.

Improper angle of the bow.   Note that the bow is not parallel with the
bridge (Fig. 3–31). This error is caused by a locked right elbow
and wrist. Unless the elbow is opened up to move freely and the
wrist moves down and out at the appropriate angle, the bow
cannot move in a straight line.

Figure 3-31

Figure 3-32

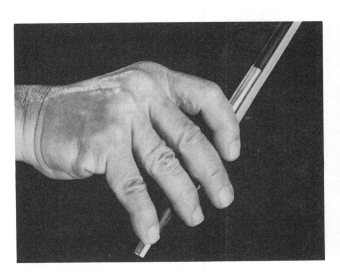

Figure 3-33

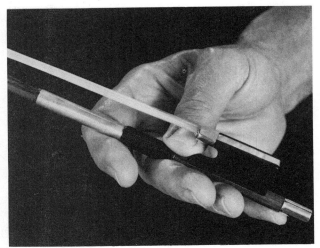

Figure 3-34

In Figure 3-32 the left elbow is not under the violin/viola and the instrument is much too low. The violin should be virtually parallel with the floor and the elbow sufficiently *under* the body of the instrument so that when playing on the "G" string for violin or "C" string for viola, the student may see the tip of the left elbow when glancing down the right side of the instrument.

Stiff fingers and thumb of right hand (Figs. 3–33 and 3–34). Notice how rigid and inflexible the fingers are. This locks the fingers and wrist and interferes with proper finger control. The student should work to *bend* the thumb and relax the fingers so that they are rounded and curve into the frog and stick.

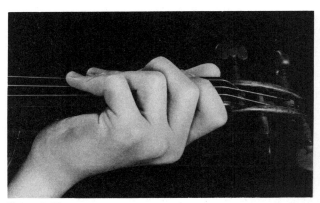

Figure 3-35

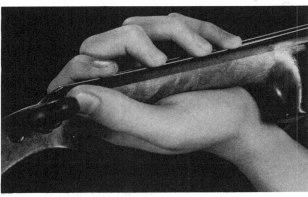

Figure 3-36

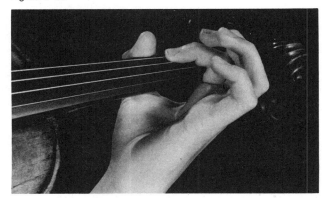

Figure 3-37

Left-hand wrist "fold" (Figs. 3–35 and 3–36). This is a common error among beginners. It should be corrected by straightening the angle of the thumb so that it points up and arching the fingers over the strings, keeping the wrist in a straight line with the arm and avoiding cramping and stiffness.

"Open palm" (Fig. 3–37). The wrist shown in the illustration is turned so that the fingers are not over the strings; this interferes with proper finger action.

Viola

All of the visual errors illustrated for the violin apply also to the viola. In addition, there are a few visual errors that can be observed when violinists change to the viola.

In general, the violist must hold his instrument lower than the violinist does in order to accommodate the larger, heavier instrument. Therefore, an adjustment must be made in the left wrist position. If the student holds the viola as in Figure 3–39, he or she should be instructed to make this adjustment as shown in Figure 3–38.

Although it is not always possible to see the adjustment in the right hand, there is a change, a shift in weight to accommodate the heavier strings of the viola. Some violists bend the

Figure 3-38

Figure 3-39

first joint of the right thumb less than on the violin bow, in order to obtain a firmer grip.

Violoncello

The "violin bow grip" (Fig. 3-40). This is a common error among students who have been taught by a violinist. The little finger should not be on top of the stick and the fingers should be more nearly perpendicular to the bow.

The "violin left hand" (Fig. 3–41). Note the incorrect angle of the fingers of the left hand in relation to the strings and the neck. The thumb and the total hand position are affected by this error. The fingers should be perpendicular to the string rather than at the violin-playing angle.

Incorrect extension (Fig. 3–42). The abuse illustrated here is caused by improper understanding of the "backward extension." Although it is correct to make this extension with a backward movement, care must be taken to adjust the fingers and the hand by a compensating downward movement so that proper hand position is maintained.

Figure 3-40

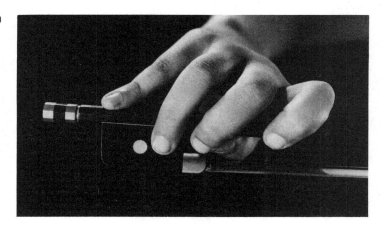

Figure 3-41

Figure 3-42

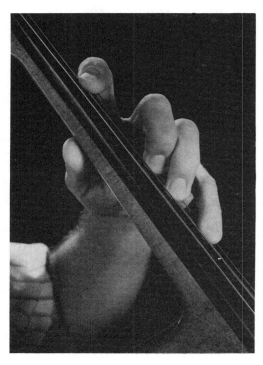

Figure 3-43

Figure 3-44

String Bass

The "violin right hand" (Fig. 3–43).   The little finger should *not* be on top of the stick, and the fingers should be completely realigned to be perpendicular to the frog. It is helpful for the teacher to suggest that the tip of the little finger be approximately where the pearl inset is on the frog.

Note also that the angle of the bow is incorrect. The bow should be somewhat parallel to the bridge.

The "violin left hand" (Fig. 3–44).   Note the improper angle of the fingers of the left hand, and the total collapse of the joints of the fingers. Obviously incorrect as this seems, it is still a common error among students who are not taught by a well-trained bass player.

Improper height and angle of the instrument (Fig. 3–46).   The bass is adjusted entirely too low, causing a poor left-hand position and improper spacing of the fingers. Figure 3–45 indicates improper angle of the bow.

When the angle of the instrument is incorrect, the student cannot cross strings properly, and his left arm moves awkwardly. Improper balance causes tension and fatigue and results in poor performance.

Often string-bass players are told to use their arms "like a pendulum," which creates the erroneous impression that the arm should be as rigid as the arm of a pendulum. The pendulum analogy causes the player to lock his right elbow, and it should be avoided (see Fig. 3–47).

Figure 3-45

Figure 3-46

Figure 3-47

40

Activities and Check List

1. In a string class, check your stand partner or neighbor on each of the position items listed on pages 34–40.
2. Look in a mirror and check yourself on each of the items listed on pages 34–40.

Self-Check List

	Yes	No
a. Is the bow at the tip at its correct angle?	☐	☐
b. Violins and violas, is the little finger of the right hand on top of the stick, thumb opposite the second finger and bent? Cellos and double basses (French bow), are your fingers perpendicular to the floor with the little finger over the frog at the first joint with the thumb bent and opposite the second finger?	☐	☐
c. Violins and violas, check your left hand. Is it collapsed or in an open-palm position? If the answer is *yes*, then correct it.	☐	☐
d. Cellos and basses, is your left wrist in a straight line with your elbow?	☐	☐

Competency 5:   Be able to tune your instrument.

Tuning Procedures

Tuning the Violin, Viola, and Cello

One of the fears that people—children and adults alike—have concerning the study of a string instrument is the matter of tuning. It is important for the teacher to make a point of dispelling this fear at the very outset. For the youngster, especially, the teacher should tune the instrument (preferably in advance of the lesson, if practical) for the first several lessons or weeks. It should be remembered that the novice wants to play the instrument. He or she needs time to get the "feel" of the instrument and become "friends," so to speak, with the new music maker. After two or three weeks the beginner should be ready to begin to explore, under the teacher's guidance, the process of tuning.

There are at least three approaches to tuning by the beginner that are in general use. Only one is to be recommended. It is important, however, to be aware of the other two approaches and understand why they are not acceptable.

One procedure to avoid, if possible, is the direct string-piano method. In this method the student tunes each string to its equivalent on the piano; that is, the A string is tuned to the same A on the piano, the D to the piano D; the G to the piano G, etc. It is natural that the student will do at home what he has observed the teacher doing, and if one could be certain that the piano at home is in tune, this procedure would not be too objectionable. However, it is well known that the piano in the typical home is not kept in tune—at least not to the degree of accuracy necessary for tuning a string instrument. If the student uses this procedure at home, he will very likely fail to get his instrument in tune. It is better that he use a good pitch pipe that possesses *the notes of all four strings.*

A second procedure, equally undesirable, is to tune the instrument to the note A on the piano, pitch pipe or A bar, and then sing downward "sol–mi–do," or "5–4–3–2–1," or the first three notes of a song that begins with a descending major triad, and so arrive at the note D. Similarly, the student sings upward from the note A ("do–mi–sol," etc.) to find the note E. Experience has shown that relying on the voice in this way will seldom result in achieving a tuning in perfect fifths.

Activities and Check List

The procedure that is recommended is as follows:

1. Allow the student several lessons or weeks to become familiar with the instrument, with the way it sounds at close range, and, above all, with the experience of playing open-string double stops in exercises so that he or she learns the unique sound of a perfect fifth.

2. At some point in the lesson, the teacher might sound the correct A on the piano, pitch pipe, or A bar, and while playing the instrument's A string, slowly turn the A tuning peg back and forth, thereby raising and lowering the pitch. The purpose of this procedure is to have the student listen and indicate when he or she thinks the two sounds produce a perfect unison. (To keep the true A sounding while the teacher does this, the student can stand at the piano and every few seconds press the A key.)

3. Once the correct A is established on the instrument, the teacher might play the open-string double-stop A–D, and by turning the D peg, slowly fluctuate the pitch. The student can then listen and indicate when the perfect fifth appears. This should be in the form of a game and can produce excitement and pleasure in a lesson.

4. When the student understands the principles involved and can identify the perfect fifth successfully, he or she is ready to experiment with these procedures alone. However, it still should be under the teacher's guidance. Much of the difficulty encountered in the early stages of learning to tune is the physical inability to maneuver the left hand while drawing the bow. Several kinds of nonslip pegs are now available, and they can be installed on any violin, viola, or cello. They aid immeasurably in facilitating the task of tuning by holding their position wherever the student stops turning (see Fig. 3-48). For some students it may be advisable in the earliest stages not to be encumbered with the complication of the bow. By holding the cello, violin, or viola between the knees and plucking the string, the student may simplify the process of pushing the peg into the peg box while adjusting the pitch, when regular pegs are used (Fig. 3-49). Bass students may also use pizzicato in the initial phases of tuning. On all string instruments it is better to loosen the string slightly and tune up to the pitch. All steel strings must have tuners. It is extremely difficult to tune steel strings accurately with pegs. Incidentally,

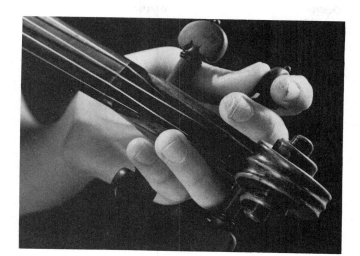

Figure 3-48

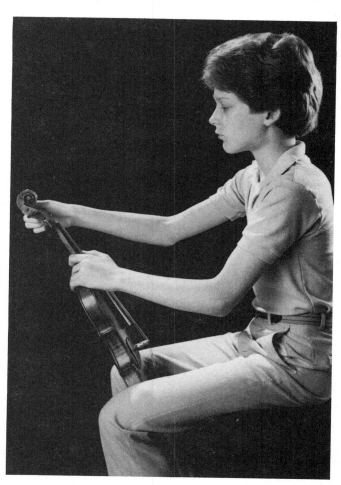

Figure 3-49

tuning can and should be utilized as an ear-training exercise. The best procedure to tuning, then, is to focus on the interval of the perfect fifth for the violin, viola, and cello. String-base students should learn to tune by harmonics as early as possible.

Self-Check List

a. Match your open strings with your neighbor's strings.

b. Violins and violas, recheck your open strings to see if you still hear perfect fifths with your left ear lifted away from the body of the instrument. Double basses and violoncellos, recheck for perfect intervals with bow.

Tuning the String Bass

The only acceptable way to tune the string bass is through the use of harmonics. There are several approaches to their use, but for accurate tuning, it is extremely difficult to rely on the open string. Once the student begins using the left hand there is no reason why he or she shouldn't experiment with finding the proper harmonics. Figure 3–50 shows the locations of harmonics on the strings.

Figure 3-50

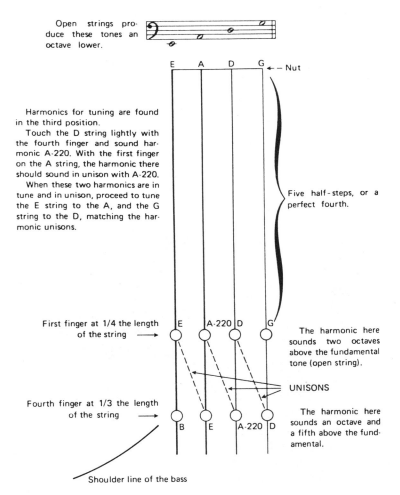

Open strings produce these tones an octave lower.

Harmonics for tuning are found in the third position.

Touch the D string lightly with the fourth finger and sound harmonic A-220. With the first finger on the A string, the harmonic there should sound in unison with A-220.

When these two harmonics are in tune and in unison, proceed to tune the E string to the A, and the G string to the D, matching the harmonic unisons.

First finger at 1/4 the length of the string →

Fourth finger at 1/3 the length of the string →

Shoulder line of the bass

Nut

Five half-steps, or a perfect fourth.

The harmonic here sounds two octaves above the fundamental tone (open string).

UNISONS

The harmonic here sounds an octave and a fifth above the fundamental.

In tuning, the student should touch the D string lightly with the fourth finger at the note A (third position, or one-third the length of the string), where it will sound the harmonic A—220. The student should adjust this note to match the A given for tuning.

Once the D string is in tune, then, still in third position, the student should play the harmonic A on the A string with the first finger (one-fourth of the string length). Caution the student not to move the hand; he or she should stay in position and touch the string lightly to produce this harmonic. The A produced on the A string should then be adjusted to match the harmonic A on the D string.

When these notes are in perfect unison, have the student move the fourth finger to the A string and produce the harmonic E (third position—one-third the length of the string). By remaining in position and lightly touching the E string with the first finger, the student will produce the same harmonic E. The student should then adjust the note until the two sounds match.

To facilitate tuning the strings on a string bass, the strings are wound to a system of gears that make tuning much easier for this instrument (see Fig. 3–51).

The same procedure is used to tune the G string. Be certain, however, that the student adjusts the G string, not the D, since the D was the string originally tuned.

An approximate guide to use in finding the fourth-finger harmonic is the fact that it is near the shoulder of the instrument (one-third the length of the string).

Good intonation is dependent on proper tuning. Learn to hear it! Learn to tune it! As a teacher, be patient but be definite in helping your students attain this accomplishment.

Figure 3-51

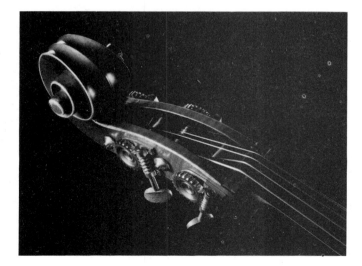

Silent Exercises to Reinforce Learning

Beginning students enjoy games.* The following may be useful to assist in developing movement in the right arm and fingers. They may be used throughout the book.

1. Exercise to develop freedom in the right arm:
   a. Ask the students to lift the bow and place it at the frog.
   b. Have them lift the bow and place it on the strings at the middle.
   c. Have them lift the bow and place it at the point.
   d. Once the students have learned to distinguish frog, middle, and point, call out instructions of bow placement and begin mixing up the sequence (middle, point, frog, point, middle, etc.).
   e. In the beginning, work at a slow, careful rate, then, since this is an exercise that may be used daily, gradually accelerate the speed of the commands until the students become proficient at the exercise.

2. Crawling exercises with the fingers of the right hand on the bow:
   a. Have the students hold the bow perpendicular to the floor with the point aimed at the ceiling. Ask them to move their fingers from the frog to the point without moving the bow. When the students are fairly proficient with this exercise, continue as follows.
   b. Ask the students to invert the bow and to aim the frog at the ceiling. Repeat the "crawling finger" exercise, this time moving the fingers from the point to the frog.
   c. Now tell the students to hold the bow in the proper hand position (parallel to the floor), and without moving the stick, make their fingers crawl from the frog to the point.
   d. Finally, have them invert the stick, so that the point is in the right hand, and let the fingers crawl from the point to the frog.

3. The teeter-totter game:
   a. With the bow hand in position, give the command "teeter-totter." The students rotate their right wrist and turn the hand over so that the palm and hair face the ceiling. This gives the teacher and student the opportunity to examine the hand for proper playing position (see self-check list).
   b. Repeat the command "teeter-totter," and the students turn the hand back to playing position.

---

*Phyllis Young in her book, *Playing the String Game*, published by the University of Texas Press, describes games that are designed "To establish the concept of a beautiful tone.... To establish the habit of making tension-free motions.... To establish an attitude that is full of confidence and free of inhibitions.... To help the student learn how to study and to achieve a sense of accomplishment.... To help nurture a love for music and the instrument."

Activities and Check List

1. Play the teeter-totter game.* At the first command with the palm facing the ceiling, check the following:

	Yes	No
a. Is the thumb against the corner of the frog and bent?	☐	☐
b. Are the thumb and second finger opposite each other?	☐	☐
c. Does the stick fall across the middle finger of the first joint?	☐	☐
d. Violins and violas, is the little finger *curved* on top of the stick?	☐	☐
Cellos and basses, is the little finger over the stick at the first joint and perpendicular to the floor?	☐	☐

2. "Teeter-totter" so that the bow is in playing position with the palm facing the floor. Check the following:

	Yes	No
a. Violins and violas, are the fingers inclined toward the tip of the bow?	☐	☐
Cellos and basses, are the fingers perpendicular to the floor?	☐	☐
b. Violins and violas, are the fingers curved with the little finger still on top of the stick?	☐	☐
Cellos and basses, are the fingers curved with the little finger aimed or covering the mother-of-pearl insert in the frog?	☐	☐

*The game does *not* apply to the double-bass German-bow position.

Playing the Instrument on the Open Strings

Competency 6:	Be able to play with a variety of bowings on the open string.

For all string instruments, the open string cycle offers an excellent format for bowing studies that are best taught by rote (see pp. 53 and 58). The cycle begins on the C string of the viola and cello and progresses through a series of fifths (G, D, and A, played by all four instruments,) to the E string of the violin and bass. After repeating the upper string, it returns to the C. Once the cycle is established, the teacher may use any combination of notes or rhythmic patterns for rote instruction. (See the nine examples on page 59.) By varying the bow speeds and by using all sections of the bow in different combinations, the student builds up a tonal base and develops right-hand facility.

A student is primarily interested in producing sound, and sound production is one of the prime functions of the right arm. Early studies should be designed to develop coordination in the bowing arm.

Introducing the Open Strings

The violin, viola, and cello are concert pitch instruments that sound as they are written and are tuned in fifths. The string bass is also a concert pitch instrument, but it is tuned in fourths and sounds an octave lower than written.

Violin. The thickest string on the violin is the G string and G is the lowest note of the instrument. The open strings progress upward in the following manner.

Viola. The thickest string on the viola is the C string and C is the lowest note of the instrument. The open strings progress upward in the following manner.

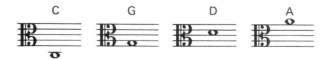

Many different bowing studies, combined with the open string cycle, should be employed (see pp. 54 and 59). The student should acquire a repertoire of bowings that can be utilized at various times to develop right-hand skills.

When the teacher introduces new material, he or she should continue to use the pizzicato in banjo style or playing position, and then arco, although of course, this may not be appropriate for all exercises or bowings.

In addition, the student should experiment with finding the proper place between the bridge and the fingerboard for the most desirable tone. Although he or she is instructed to put the bow midway between the bridge and the fingerboard, the best point for beautiful tone will vary with different instruments. Determination of the best sounding point also changes with the speed and pressure of the bow and with changes in the string length.

Violoncello. The thickest string on the violoncello is the C string, and C is the lowest note of the instrument. The open strings progress upward in the following manner.

String bass. The thickest string on the string bass is the E string, and this is usually the lowest *string* on the instrument, although special extensions make it possible for professionals to play lower notes. Beginning with the E, the open strings progress upward in the following manner.

| Competency 7: | Be able to play pizzicato. |

Pizzicato

The Italian word *pizzicato* (abbreviation "pizz.") indicates that the player is to pluck the string with the finger. This technique produces a unique sound effect; it also is useful in the early stages of learning to play a string instrument. By using pizzicato, the performer is relieved of any bowing problems while learning the notes of a piece. The following procedure is suggested.

Place the bow on the music stand. Now form the right hand as shown in Figure 4–1, with the thumb and first finger extended and the second, third, and fourth fingers curved into the palm of the hand.

Figure 4-1

Figure 4-2

Using Figure 4-2 as a model, place the fleshy part of the thumb against the fingerboard with the first finger well extended over the strings, about two inches from the large end of the fingerboard on the violin and a proportional distance on the larger string instruments. At all times during early pizzicato playing, keep the thumb anchored against the fingerboard. This provides a base for accuracy in the selection of strings. To hold the string in plucking, use only the fleshy part near the end of the first finger. The pulling motion should be from the side, not downward. (Cellos see Figure 4-4, and bass players see Figures 4-5 and 4-6.)

If the entire piece (or exercise) is to be played pizzicato, the bow can remain on the music stand, thereby freeing the right hand completely. At other times, however, the bow must remain in the right hand. It can be held with the second, third, and fourth fingers, with the thumb and first finger extended. See Figures 4-3, 4-4, 4-5, and 4-6.

The pizzicato technique is useful in many ways in class teaching. While working on a piece (or a special technical problem), the teacher might let each student take turns performing separately with the bow while the rest of the class plays pizzicato. This not only affords each student the challenge (and thrill) of appearing as "soloist," but also gives the teacher an opportunity to study and evaluate the progress of each student. At the same time, all the other students are kept busy getting additional practice, which they welcome, since they know that it will soon be their turn to be "soloist" with the bow.

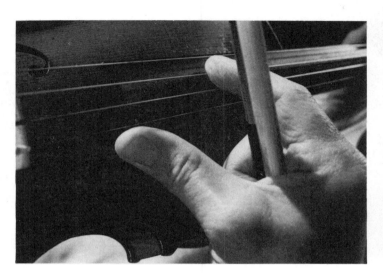

Figure 4-3

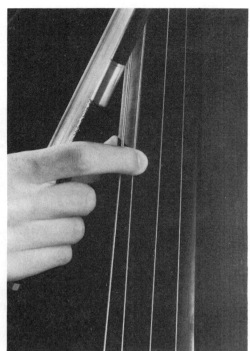

Figure 4-4

Figure 4-5

Figure 4-6

Another effective use of pizzicato is to give variety and length to a piece for recital or concert purposes. As soon as the class has learned three or four pieces, regardless of how short or elementary the pieces may seem, an appearance of some kind is desirable. This not only demonstrates to others (fellow classmates, parents, and teachers) the progress that is being made, but provides a tremendous incentive for individual practice. A simple piece of only 16 measures, for example, can easily be made into a full-length concert piece in the following manner: first time, tutti with bow (arco); second time, tutti–pizzicato; third time, solo or duet with pizzicato accompaniment; fourth time, tutti with bow. If the piece is in two parts, the possibilities for variety are even greater.

Activity and Check List

1. Practice going from arco to pizzicato and back to arco 10 times.

Self-Check List	Yes	No
a. Is your thumb against the fingerboard when plucking?	☐	☐
b. Are you plucking with the fleshy part of the tip of the finger?	☐	☐

The Open String Cycle

⊓ is the symbol for "down-bow." (*Pull* the bow from the frog to the tip.) ∨ is the symbol for "up-bow." (*Push* the bow from the tip to the frog.)
See page 49 for instructions on pizzicato. Pizzicato may be performed either banjo style or in playing position.

Bowing Studies:

1. Use the middle of the bow.
2. Use the upper half of the bow.
3. Use the lower half of the bow.
4. Use all three sections of the bow, staccato.
5. Play the entire cycle "down-bow," returning to the frog after each note:

6. Play the entire cycle "up-bow," returning to the point after each note:

7. Play the cycle spiccato (bouncing bow—see page 168) with the lower half of the bow:

Activities and Check List

1. Name the open strings and put them in their proper place on a staff. (Check your text.)
2. Describe the following terms and symbols: ⊓ , ∨ , arco, staccato.

Swing Your Partner

Slovakian Folk Song

Gavotte

F. S. Gossec

Bowing Studies on the Open String Cycle

Bowing Studies:

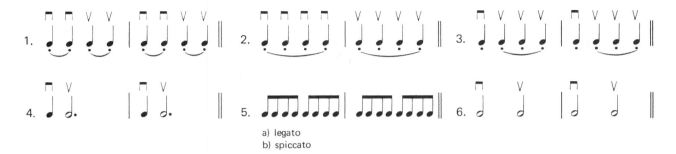

a) legato
b) spiccato

A bouncing bow moves like a staccato except that it is "off" the string instead of remaining on the string. The bow arm should be relaxed as it moves in a rocking motion with the bow striking at the bottom point of this movement.

Double Stops

Double stops are used because they amplify the string tone. In addition, playing double stops helps to develop a desirable string tone, since it cannot be done without "rubbing" the bow against the strings. Beginners tend to allow the bow to slide, producing a "glassy" tone, but double-stop playing requires a good "pull" and "push." Another advantage is that this kind of practice will eventually lead to smoother string crossings.

The Open String Cycle for Double Stops

Music for Double Stops

College Song

Folk Song

Learning Unit 5

Finger Patterns One and Two

Competency 8:	Be able to play songs with a variety of bowings in the first finger pattern.

The finger-pattern approach enables students to begin playing in a variety of keys at the very beginning of their instruction. The fingers of the left hand are not locked in any one pattern and facility is developed through movement. Materials that utilize only one key or one finger pattern for extended periods of time create false concepts.

The First Finger Pattern

Finger patterns are based on a five-note scale sequence on the open string. Thus, the first finger pattern is the tonic tetrachord of the major scale beginning with the open string (*do, re, mi, fa, sol*). It consists of the normal progression of two whole steps, a half step, and a whole step. In addition to forming the first five notes of the major scale, this finger pattern seems to be the most comfortable, natural position for the fingers of the left hand.

On the violin or viola, the distance from one finger to the next represents either a whole step or a half step. For a half step, the adjacent fingers usually touch each other. For a whole step, the adjacent fingers are spread apart. Plucking and listening for the correct pitch will determine the exact distance between the fingers. With the instrument under the right arm (banjo style), place the fingers in half steps and whole steps on the string and determine the correct spacing while plucking with the thumb of the right hand.

The first finger pattern for the violin or viola is as follows (see Fig. 5–1).

Awareness of key is basic to music instruction, and instrumental training should develop the tonal sense. Students of string instruments should learn the vocabulary of music from the beginning so that it will be a part of their working knowledge and skills.

$$(0-1-\overset{\frown}{2}\ 3-4)$$

open string ⟶ whole step
first finger ⟶ whole step
second finger ⟶ half-step (∧)
third finger ⟶ whole step
fourth finger

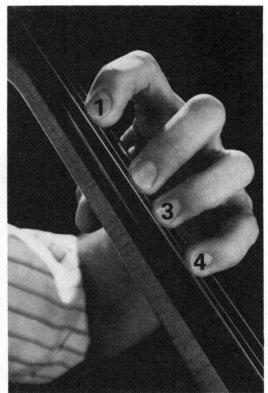

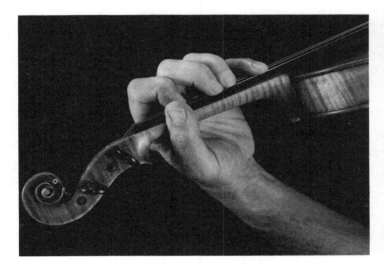

Figure 5-1   Figure 5-2

The second and third fingers, which constitute the half step (from *mi* to *fa*), practically touch each other. The degree of contact will vary according to the individual finger thickness and the string length.

On the cello, each finger represents a *half step*. To play a whole step at this stage, one must skip a finger. Thus, a whole step from the first finger would be the third finger. Since it is desirable to keep as many fingers as possible on the string, the intervening finger is also placed on the string.

The first finger pattern for the cello is as follows (see Fig. 5–2):

$$(0{-}1{-}\overset{\frown}{3}\ 4{-}0)$$

open string ⟍
      ⟋ whole step
first finger ⟍
      ⟋ whole step
third finger ⟍
      ⟋ half-step (⌢)
fourth finger ⟍
      ⟋ whole step
adjacent open string ⟋

On the string bass, the span of all four fingers represents a whole step. The first finger pattern for string bass is as follows (see Fig. 5–3):

$$(0\!-\!1\!-\!\widehat{4}\ \widehat{0}\!-\!1)$$

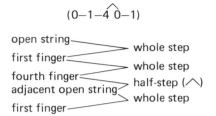

Figure 5-3

Activities and Check List

1. Place the fingers silently on the string in the first finger pattern. (Violins and violas, hold the instrument banjo style, watching where the fingers fall.)
2. Play the fingers pizzicato.
3. Violin and viola, do the above on all four strings. Violoncello and double bass, do the above only on the lower three strings.
4. Play the pattern arco.
5. Practice the first-finger-patterns material on pages 66–68.

Self-Check List

	Yes	No
a. Sing a major scale from the tonic to the dominant (do–sol) beginning with the open string. As you pluck each note when playing the first finger pattern, does each pitch match what you are singing?	☐	☐
b. When step one is fairly accurate, play arco. Does each note match the notes you sang?	☐	☐
c. Violins and violas, are your fingers perpendicular to the strings and slightly arched so that you are pressing down with the fleshy part of your finger tip?	☐	☐
Violoncellos, are your fingers perpendicular to the strings and slightly arched so that you are pressing down with the fleshy part on the inside part, *not the tip*, of the finger?	☐	☐
Double basses, are your fingers perpendicular to the strings with your first finger pointed at a 45 degree angle toward the ceiling and the little finger pointing slightly down toward the floor?	☐	☐

Music Exercises and Pieces in the First Finger Pattern

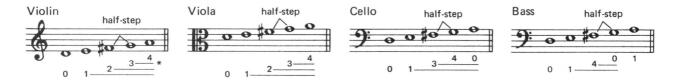

1. Practice playing the above patterns pizzicato. Violin and viola players should practice them in banjo style as well as in playing position.
2. Experiment by placing the fingers in the first finger pattern on each of the other three strings of each instrument.

*An extender indicates that the finger should be held down for the duration of the line.

Do the entire exercise, including the bowing studies, on the G string. (String bass may do so with shifts or remain tacit.) W.B. is an abbreviation for "whole bow."

Bowing Exercise on First Finger Pattern

Bowing Studies:

1. Spiccato at the frog

2. Staccato (upper half and lower half of the bow)

3.

4.
   a) legato (middle of the bow)
   b) spiccato at the frog

5.
   a) legato (middle of the bow)
   b) spiccato (middle of the bow)

6.
   Return to frog on ⊓

7.
   Return to point on V

8.

9. fr. W.B. pt. W.B.   fr. W.B. pt. W.B.

10.

11.

Continue to employ these bowings whenever applicable, such as in new finger patterns and scales.

"Zipping"

As a student begins to use the fingers of the left hand, he or she tends to grip the neck of the instrument. To relieve this tension, several exercises should be employed regularly.

"Zipping," which is placing the second finger lightly on a string and just sliding it up and down the neck, producing a "siren" sound, is one device to prevent a tense grip. If a student is gripping the neck of the instrument, his thumb will not move freely. In violin and viola playing, zipping may also reveal how well the student is holding the instrument with the jaw. Unless the jaw is holding the instrument securely, the left hand is not free to move.

"Tapping"

Another technique to improve hand position is to tap the strings silently with all four fingers of the left hand in various positions (first position, third position, etc.), or at various points on the different strings. This develops mobility in hand movement, which is so essential to proper string playing.*

These exercises should be done daily with other silent drills.

*See *Action Studies* by Paul Rolland, published by Boosey & Hawkes, 1978.

Chorale

Johann Sebastian Bach

It is of utmost importance that the proper portion of the bow be used for the maximum effect. The point or frog must be used as indicated in the music.

Hold Up Your Petticoats

Part Playing in the First Finger Pattern

Ensemble playing is a highly effective means of developing independence in playing. Almost any combination of instruments may be used in a duet, trio, etc. The Humperdinck duet given here may be played by members of the same family (for example, as a violin duet), or it may be played by a combination of instruments, such as the basses on part I and the violas on part II. It is a good idea to experiment with every possible combination.

Excerpt from "Hansel and Gretel"

Engelbert Humperdinck

*U.H.—upper half of the bow; L.H.—lower half.

<table>
<tr><td>Competency 9:</td><td>Be able to play songs with a variety of bowings in the second finger pattern.</td></tr>
</table>

The Second Finger Pattern

The second finger pattern is based on the tonic tetrachord of the natural minor scale, beginning with the open string (*la, ti, do, re, mi*). It consists of the normal progression of a whole step, a half step, and two whole steps.

The second finger pattern for the viola or violin is as follows (see Fig. 5–4):

$$(0-\widehat{1\ 2}-3-4)$$

open string ⎯⎯⎯⎯ whole step
first finger ⎯⎯⎯⎯ half-step (⌢)
second finger ⎯⎯⎯⎯ whole step
third finger ⎯⎯⎯⎯ whole step
fourth finger

Figure 5-4

The second finger pattern for the cello is as follows (see Fig. 5–5):

$$(0-\widehat{1\ 2}-4-0)$$

open string ⎯⎯⎯⎯ whole step
first finger ⎯⎯⎯⎯ half-step (⌢)
second finger ⎯⎯⎯⎯ whole step
fourth finger ⎯⎯⎯⎯ whole step
adjacent open string

Figure 5-5   Figure 5-6

The second finger pattern for the string bass is as follows (see Fig. 5–6):

$$(0-\widehat{1\ 2}-0-1)$$

open string ——————— whole step
first finger ———————
second finger (extended) —— half-step (⌒)
—— whole step
adjacent open string ——————
—— whole step
first finger ———————

Activities and Check List

1. Place the fingers silently on the string in the second finger pattern. (Violins and violas, hold the instrument banjo style, watching where the fingers fall.)
2. Play the patterns pizzicato.
3. Violins and violas, do the above on all four strings. Cellos and double basses, do the above only on the three lower strings.
4. Play the pattern arco.

5. Practice the second finger pattern on pages 78-80.

Self-Check List

		Yes	No
a.	Sing a natural minor scale from the tonic to the dominant (la–mi) beginning with the open string being used. As you pluck each note when playing the second finger pattern, does each pitch match what you are singing?	☐	☐
b.	When step one is fairly accurate, play arco. Does each pitch match the notes you sang?	☐	☐
c.	Violins and violas, are your left fingers curved so that you are playing on the fleshy part of your finger tip?	☐	☐
	Violoncellos, are your fingers perpendicular to the strings and slightly arched so that you are pressing down with the fleshy part on the *inside, not the tip*, of the finger?	☐	☐
	Double basses, are your fingers perpendicular to the strings with your first finger pointed at a 45 degree angle toward the ceiling and the little finger pointing slightly down toward the floor in line with your elbow?	☐	☐

Music Exercise and Pieces for the First and Second Finger Patterns

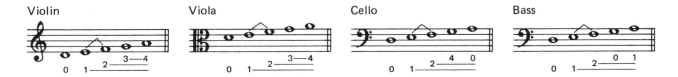

1. Practice playing the above patterns pizzicato. Violin and viola players should practice them in banjo style as well as in playing position.
2. Experiment by placing the fingers in the second finger pattern on each of the other three strings of each instrument.

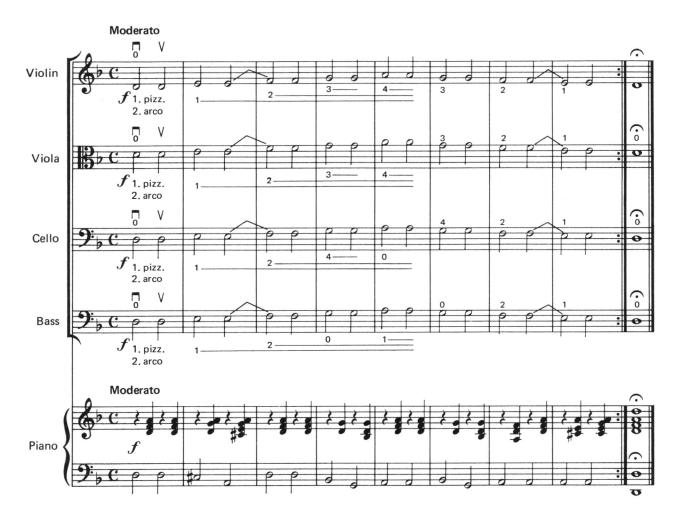

Madrigal

Encina/Klotman

Amaryllis
(First Finger Pattern)

Louis XIII (1601-1643)

* ⸗ means semi-staccato.

Learning Unit 6
Slurs and Double Stops Using Patterns One and Two

Competency 10:	Be able to play bowing with slurs.

Slurs

It is not uncommon to find that students may at first have a little difficulty in coordinating their hands and fingers when using slurs. To establish the concept of a slur (two or more notes on the same bow, i.e., the bow continuing in the same direction while changing notes), it may be best to begin by playing the open string cycle with a short pause between each note. Once the idea is established, it is easier for students to combine the left and right hands in the use of slurs.

Slurs (Open Strings)

Two notes on a bow

Repeat on the G and A strings using the first and second finger patterns.

Activities and Check List

1. Play exercise with slurs on the open strings. (See pp. 83–87.)
2. Repeat the exercises only begin on the lowest string and proceed to the top string individually.
3. Play exercises and songs on pages 84–89.

Self-Check List

	Yes	No
a. Does the bow move parallel to the bridge when playing the above exercise?	☐	☐
b. Is the bow divided equally in the above exercise?	☐	☐

Slurs (Four on a Bow)

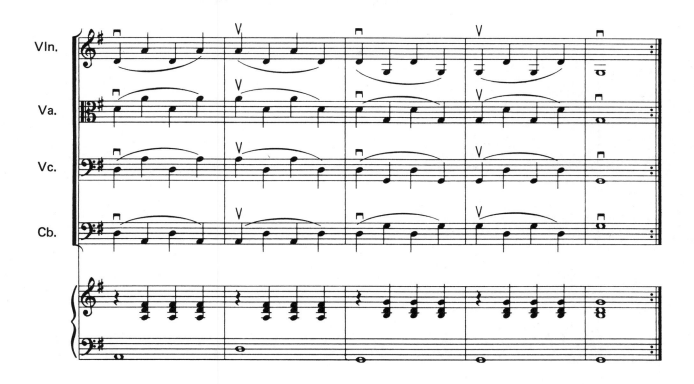

This composition utilizes combinations of the first and second finger patterns.

Bourrée

Johann Sebastian Bach

*Scales and arpeggios are the basis for most of our Western music. They serve as a medium by which most technique is developed, and they provide the best material for early ear training, particularly for establishing a sense of tonality. To make the study of scales more interesting, a variety of bowing and rhythmic studies should be utilized.

Competency 11:	Be able to play double stops combining fingers with an open string.

Crossing Strings and Double Stops

In the following exercise, the students begin to combine concepts. The first exercise involves "crossing strings" and it is of the utmost importance to keep the fingers down on the upper string through each crossing. This requirement is reinforced in the "double-stop" exercise, since the student cannot play a double stop correctly unless the fingers are kept down. In addition, the student becomes more acutely aware of intonation, since it is required to play a scale with a pedal point; the pedal tone must be kept constant and each note of the scale must be tuned against it. When crossing strings, it is well to emphasize keeping the left fingers down as much as possible. This will not only facilitate a smoother crossing but also will assist in developing better left-hand technique.

Because of the bowing angle of the violin and viola, which moves somewhat perpendicular to the ground, when going from a lower string to an upper string begin with a down-bow. The cello and bass bows move parallel to the ground so that it is better, because of the arm and wrist movement, to begin with an up-bow when going from a *lower* string to an *upper* string. This applies mainly to a sequence of alternating notes as found in the next exercise. However, do not forget that we are applying this principle to *strings* and not to *pitches*, so that on the string bass the open G is higher than the open D and therefore begins with a down-bow.

Crossing Strings

Double Stops

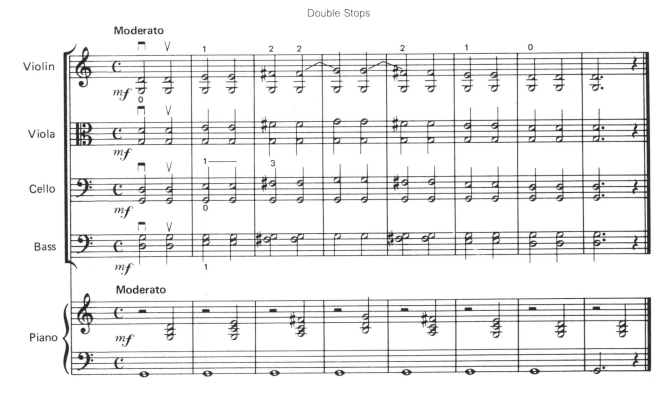

Crossing Strings
(Second Finger Pattern)

Double Stops

Activities and Check List

1. Practice playing 1/8 notes in the middle of the bow alternating open strings. (i.e. G–D–G–D, etc.) Violins, violas, and basses begin with a ⊓ bow while cellos begin with a V bow.
2. Practice the above activity at the point and at the frog.
3. Play exercises on pages 91 and 92.

Self-Check List

	Yes	No
a. As you play the above activities does the bow remain parallel to the bridge?	☐	☐
b. Is the wrist of the right hand moving in a relaxed motion and not rigid and stiff?	☐	☐

Finger Patterns Three, Four, and Five

Competency 12:	Be able to play songs with a variety of bowings in the third finger pattern.

The Third Finger Pattern

The third finger pattern is based on the scale beginning with the third note of the major scale (*mi, fa, sol, la, ti*). Thus, the half step occurs between the open string and the first finger. Since this involves a finger extension for the cello, begin the scale pattern with the *upper note*, so that the player executes the extension of the first finger in a backward movement. (The octave is used to establish the correct pitch and to set the hand position as shown in Figure 7–1.)

Figure 7–1

This extension principle is essential to proper finger placement for the left hand on the cello. Too often heterogeneous string books introduce this first extension, the whole step between first and second fingers, by indicating that the second finger moves *down*. This is *incorrect!* In the beginning, the proper way to employ this whole step is a backward movement, or extension, of the first finger. In the process, the player drops the point of the elbow so that the hand is able to retain the same relative position and shape. The forward extension is another type of movement and is introduced later.

For the string bass (see Fig. 7–2), the entire hand moves one half step back which lowers the pitch, and keeps the same finger relationship used in the first finger pattern, that is,

$$0\text{--}0\text{--}4\text{--}\widehat{1}\,0.$$

Figure 7–2

This, incidentally, is the half position for the string bass. (There is no "extended position" for the bass as there is for the cello. The normal hand position for the bass incorporates this extension.)

For the violin and viola (see Fig. 7–3), the interval spacing, beginning with the top note, is as follows:

$$4{-}3{-}2{-}\widehat{1\ 0}.$$

Figure 7-3

For the cello (see Fig. 7–1), the fingers are spaced as follows:

$$0{-}4{-}2{-}\widehat{1\ 0}.$$

Activities and Checklist

1. Place the fingers silently on the string in the third finger pattern. (Violins and violas, hold the instrument banjo style, watching where the fingers fall.)
2. Play the patterns pizzicato.
3. Violins and violas, do the above on all four strings. Cellos and double basses, do the above only on the three lower strings.
4. Play the pattern arco.
5. Practice the third-finger-pattern exercises and pieces on pages 98-101.

Self-Check List

	Yes	No
a. Sing a natural minor scale from the tonic to the dominant (la–mi) beginning with the open string being used. As you pluck each note when playing the third finger pattern does each pitch match what you are singing?	☐	☐
b. When step one is fairly accurate, play arco. Does each pitch match the notes you sang?	☐	☐

c. Violins and violas, are your left fingers curved so that you are playing on the fleshy part of your finger tip? □ □

Violoncellos, are your fingers perpendicular to the strings and slightly arched so that you are pressing down with the fleshy part on the *inside, not the tip* of the finger? □ □

Double basses, are your fingers perpendicular to the strings with the first finger pointed at a 45 degree angle toward the ceiling and the little finger pointing slightly down toward the floor in line with your elbow? □ □

Exercises and Pieces in the Third Finger Pattern

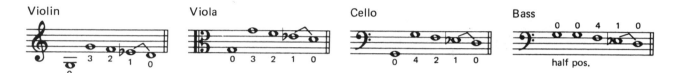

1. Practice playing the above patterns pizzicato. Violin and viola players should practice them in banjo style as well as in playing position.
2. Experiment by placing the fingers in the third finger pattern on each of the other three strings of each instrument.

Melody

Robert Klotman

Hatikvah

Israeli Song

In the "Little Owl" you will encounter chromatic passages. The violin and viola will need to *slide* the finger indicated to the adjoining half step, in this piece to the lower half step. The cello and string bass will use the appropriate half-step fingering. (It will involve moving the hand—shifting.)

Chromatic Scales
(To be practiced separately in homogeneous groupings)

Violin

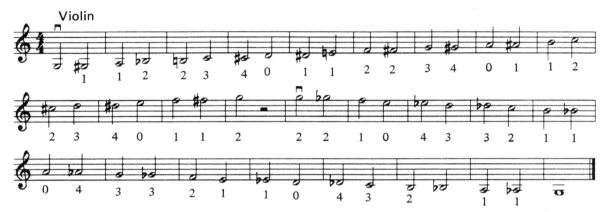

Viola

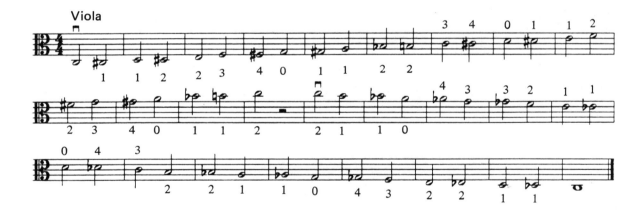

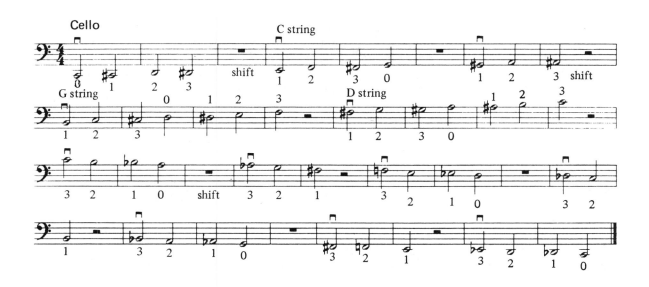

The Little Owl

Robert Schumann, Op. 79, No. 10

The Fourth Finger Pattern

The fourth finger pattern is based on the tetrachord beginning on the seventh note of the major scale (*ti, do, re, mi, fa*). It consists of a half step, two whole steps, and a half step.

On the violin and viola, to move from the third finger pattern to the fourth finger pattern, students need only lower the fourth finger a half step so that it touches the third finger. Thus, we have (see Fig. 7–4).

$$\widehat{0\,1}-2-\widehat{3\,4}.$$

Figure 7–4

For the cello, the fourth finger pattern involves a half step between the open string and the first finger, and it uses the same principle as established in the third finger pattern, that is, the fact that the extension is a backward movement. Note that there are octave jumps in the early stages of study, in order to avoid use of the extended fourth finger, which later will be handled through shifts and advanced extension. See Figure 7–5.

On the string bass, the same principle applies for the fourth finger pattern as for the third finger pattern, that is, (see Fig. 7–6):

$$(\widehat{0\,1}-4-\widehat{0\,1}).$$

Figure 7-5

Figure 7-6

Exercises and Pieces in the Fourth Finger Pattern

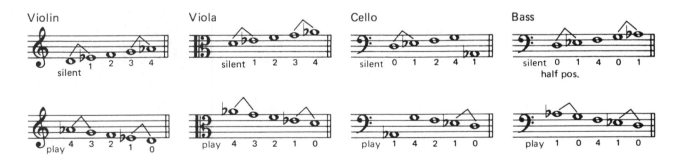

Violin
silent   1   2   3   4

Viola
silent   1   2   3   4

Cello
silent   0   1   2   4   1

Bass
silent   0   1   4   0   1
half pos.

play   4   3   2   1   0

play   4   3   2   1   0

play   1   4   2   1   0

play   1   0   4   1   0

Practice playing the above patterns pizzicato (banjo style) and arco.

The following piece, "Prayer from Zampa," is arranged so that any of the string instruments, with the exception of the string bass, can perform it as a solo with a string-orchestra accompaniment. The accompaniment is supplied by independent parts, providing a full ensemble effect. This kind of material is excellent for demonstrations at P.T.A., administrator's meetings, etc.

Before playing this piece as written, practice playing it with a separate bow to each note.

Prayer from "Zampa"
(Solo or String Ensemble)

Louis-Joseph-Ferdinand Hérold

This material may be used for musical programs or for performances whenever the opportunity arises.

The C harmonic minor arpeggio given here utilizes the fourth finger pattern. It is excellent preparation for the song, "Dark Eyes."

C Minor Arpeggios

Dark Eyes

Gypsy Melody

*Move the finger forward a half step.

*Move the finger forward a half-step.

Activities and Check List

1. Place the fingers silently on the string in the fourth finger pattern. (Violins and violas, hold the instrument banjo style, watching where the fingers fall.)
2. Play the patterns pizzicato.
3. Violins and violas, do the above on all four strings. Cellos and double basses, do the above only on the three lower strings.
4. Play the pattern arco.
5. Practice the fourth-finger-pattern exercises and pieces on pages 108–113.

Self-Check List

	Yes	No
a. Sing a natural major scale from the seventh to the subdominant (ti–fa) beginning with the open string being used. As you pluck each note when playing the fourth finger pattern does each pitch match what you are singing?	☐	☐
b. When step one is fairly accurate, play arco. Does each pitch match the notes you sang?	☐	☐
c. Violins and violas, are your left fingers curved so that you are playing on the fleshy part of your finger tip?	☐	☐
Violoncellos, are your fingers perpendicular to the strings and slightly arched so that you are pressing down with the fleshy part on the *inside, not the tip* of the finger?	☐	☐
Double basses, are your fingers perpendicular to the strings with the first finger pointed at a 45 degree angle toward the ceiling and the little finger pointing slightly down toward the floor in line with your elbow?	☐	☐

Competency 14:   Be able to play songs with a variety of bowings in the fifth finger pattern.

The Fifth Finger Pattern

The fifth finger pattern is based on the tetrachord beginning on the fourth note of the major scale (*fa, sol, la, ti, do*).

The intervals on the violin and viola are as follows (see Fig. 7-7).

$$(0-1-2-\overset{\frown}{3\ 4})$$

open string ———————————————— whole step
first finger ———————————————— whole step
second finger ———————————————— whole step
third finger ——————————————— half-step (∧)
fourth finger

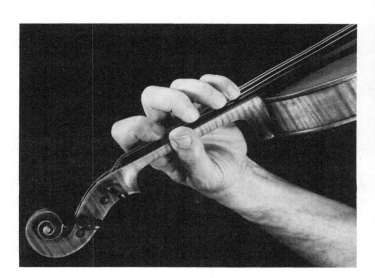

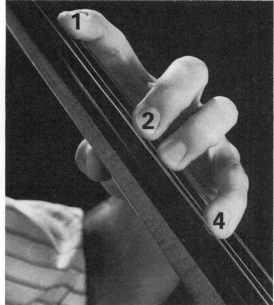

Figure 7-7   Figure 7-8

The fifth finger pattern for the cello (see Fig. 7-8) is as follows:

$$(0-1-2-\overset{\frown}{4\ 0})$$

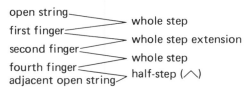

open string ———————————————— whole step
first finger ———————————————— whole step extension
second finger ———————————————— whole step
fourth finger ——————————————— half-step (∧)
adjacent open string

Figure 7–9

Figure 7–10

In this pattern, the thumb of the left hand is in the same position in relation to the second finger as it was in the third finger pattern; that is, the first finger is extended backward.

The fifth finger pattern for the string bass (see Figs. 7–9 and 7–10) uses both the first position and the half position. Begin in the first position and move to the half position on the note that raises the open string. See the fingering given in the accompanying exercise on the A major scale.

[0—1—4—1 (half pos.) 2].

Practice playing the above patterns pizzicato (banjo style) and arco.

Exercises and Pieces in the Fifth Finger Pattern

Shenandoah

Activities and Check List

1. Place the fingers silently on the string in the fifth finger pattern. (Violins and violas, hold the instrument banjo style, watching where the fingers fall.)
2. Play the patterns pizzicato.
3. Violins and violas, do the above on all four strings. Cellos and double basses, do the above only on the lower three strings.
4. Play the pattern arco.
5. Practice the fifth-finger-pattern exercises and pieces on pages 117–118.

Self-Check List

	Yes	No
a. Sing a major scale from the fourth to the tonic (fa–do) beginning with the open string being used. As you pluck each note when playing the fifth finger pattern does each pitch match what you are singing?	☐	☐
b. When step one is fairly accurate, play arco. Does each pitch match the notes you sang?	☐	☐
c. Violins and violas, are left fingers curved so that you are playing on the fleshy part of your finger tip?	☐	☐
Violoncellos, are your fingers perpendicular to the strings and slightly arched so that you are pressing down with the fleshy part on the *inside, not the tip* of the finger?	☐	☐
Double basses, are your fingers perpendicular to the strings with the first finger pointed at a 45 degree angle toward the ceiling and the little finger pointing slightly down toward the floor in line with your elbow?	☐	☐

Part III
Solos, Études, and Ensembles

Playing Solos, Ensembles, and Études in All Patterns

Competency 15:	Be able to utilize all of the five finger patterns in a variety of pieces.

One of the best ways to promote a string program is to have beginners perform and demonstrate how quickly they can acquire enough skill to enjoy what they are doing. This helps to allay some of the concerns regarding the so-called extreme difficulties of learning to play string instruments. Performing solos gives an excellent device for motivating students to practice. The Chorale from Finlandia on page 124 is arranged so that every member of the string class may be soloist with proper string accompaniment. This arrangement provides incentive, challenge, and pleasure for the soloist and for the entire class as well. The discipline involved in providing an accompaniment is helpful in the students' musical development. It is important for them to learn to listen and to follow a solo line. Finlandia may also be played as an ensemble using various combinations of instruments.

Activities and Check List

1. Play pages 124–128. The first time through, have everyone play part I.
2. The second time through, divide the class or individuals into first and second parts.
3. The third time, switch parts.

Self-Check List

	Yes	No
a. If you are playing the first part, can you hear the second part in all the instruments?	☐	☐
b. If you are playing the second part, can you hear part I in instruments other than your own?	☐	☐
c. Are you observing the bowings as printed?	☐	☐

Chorale from "Finlandia"

Jean Sibelius

A Minor Scale (Melodic)

Farewell, Minka

Russian Folk Song

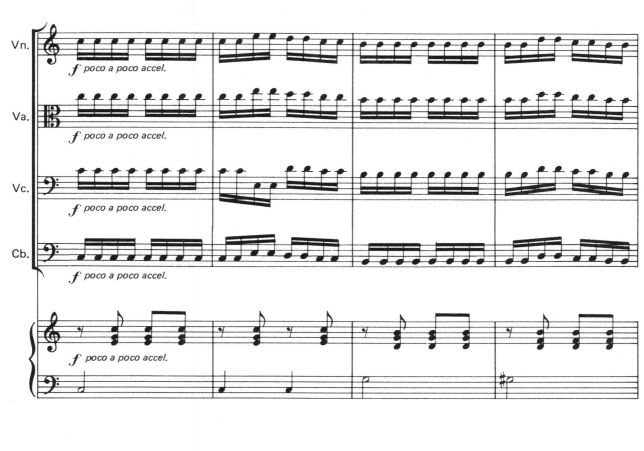

Activities and Check List

1. The studies on page 129 explore further the bowing technique of spiccato. The spiccato is an off-the-string bowing motion that follows the same movement or direction as the detaché bowing (see p. 168). However, the arm is completely relaxed so that the stick is free to bounce of its own accord. Once the "feel" of the stick's bounce is acquired, controlled bowings may be employed, following the scale pattern. Students and teachers should create bowing studies of their own, based on the scale, to practice in addition to those given here.

2. The scale and bowing studies are to be used as preparation for "Farewell, Minka," a Russian folk song. The variations utilize different styles such as legato, pizzicato, and hooked détaché, and the rhythms are designed to develop bow control and speed.

3. The "theme and variation" is an excellent form for instruction purposes. It introduces variety into a repetitive idea. Students soon have the basic musical ideal fixed in their ears and minds. They can then concentrate on developing the skills required for each variation.

Self-Check List

	Yes	No
a. When playing the scale spiccato, is your arm sufficiently relaxed so that the spring of the bow or the stick practically bounces itself?	☐	☐
b. Are you practicing the scale with all of the bowing studies listed at the bottom of the scale exercise?	☐	☐
c. Make a cassette tape recording of your own performance of "Farewell, Minka." Does it sound enjoyable to you?	☐	☐

German Dance

Joseph Haydn

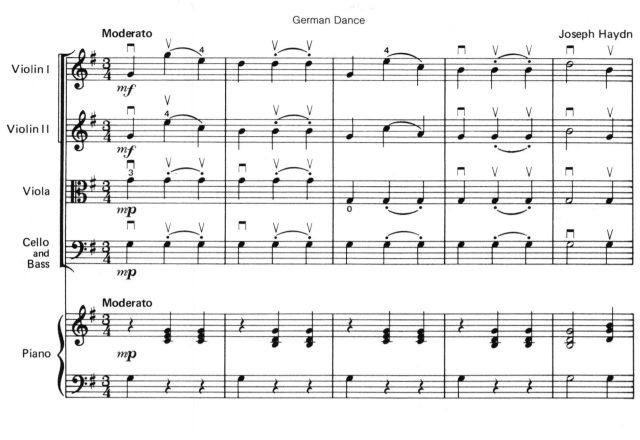

Chorale

Robert Schumann

Trio from Symphony No. 39

Wolfgang Amadeus Mozart

This is a review of combinations of the first, second, and third finger patterns. See directions on pages 62–64, 75–76, and 95–97.

Gavotte

Padre Giambattista Martini

America the Beautiful
(Duet)

Samuel A. Ward

Theme from the "New World" Symphony

Antonin Dvořák

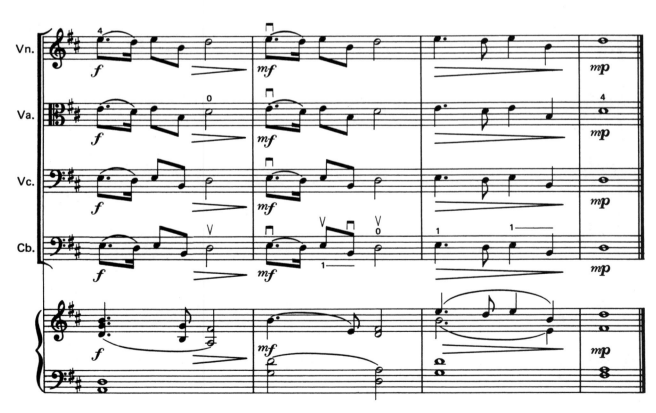

Entr'acte

March from "Scipio"

George Frederick Handel

*Extend the fourth finger one half step.

March from "Alceste"

Christoph Willibald Gluck

Activity and Check List

1. Select a composition from pages 137–157 and prepare it for performance in class. (If necessary arrange with other students who may not be in this class to fill out the ensemble for this performance.) Invite the class to serve as a panel of judges.

Check List

	Yes	No
a. Were the parts well balanced in performance so you could hear each part?	☐	☐
b. Did the student produce a proper string sound on the instrument?	☐	☐
c. Did the performers demonstrate proper playing position?	☐	☐
d. Was it a musical performance rather than just another exercise?	☐	☐

Part IV
Intermediate Class Instruction

Some Simple Guidelines Determining Bowing

By now it should be evident that the string player's technique is in direct proportion to the development of his bow arm. All of the previous studies contain a variety of bowing exercises intended to free the right arm from rigidity and to develop correct phrasing and good tone.

There are several schools of bowing, each taking an arbitrary position on its own advantages. Since the bow works either with or against gravity, and more strength is attainable close to the hand than at the point, we advocate the principle that more hair and greater pull can be applied as the bow moves from the frog to the tip. This idea comes from the Russian school, in which string players are taught to begin the "down-bow" using only part of the bow hair at the frog, with the stick turned so that the *hair is toward the bridge*. Then the bow is gradually turned so that the hair is flat against the string beyond the middle portion of the bow.

Basically, the turning or flattening is determined by the quality of sound, the distribution of the bow according to musical demands, and the stick balance. When selecting bowings for music, the player should be governed by technical and artistic demands as well as style, period, and taste. These criteria are important factors in the choice of bowing for a particular exercise or piece of music.

Basic Principles of Bowing

In performance a string player generally begins measures with a down-bow (⊓). Thus, if a composition or phrase begins with a single note on the last beat of a measure, the note is played with an up-bow (∨). A simple formula to follow is this: If there is an even number of notes before a barline, the player should begin with a down-bow; if there is an odd number, he should begin with an up-bow.

Accents are achieved best at the frog with a down-bow. Likewise, chords marked *forte* are more effective with a down-bow, but this, of course, will depend on the tempo and character of the music.

Since accents are played with a down-bow, unaccented notes are played with an up-bow, and consequently, afterbeats are frequently played with up-bows. The same basic principle of accented notes applies to syncopation. Since the accent falls off the beat, it should be played, if at all possible, with a down-bow:

On bowings that cross back and forth on the strings without slurs, the upper note should begin with a down-bow on the cello and bass but with an up-bow on the violin and viola. The reverse is true in those bowings that cross strings without slurs and that begin on a lower string; that is, the bottom note on the violin or viola begins with a down-bow, while on the cello and bass it is an up-bow.

When bowing is not specifically indicated, a combination of dotted eighth and sixteenth is generally played as a hooked bowing:

Incidentally, hooked bowings are used frequently to achieve many of the effects mentioned above; they permit the performer to arrive at the proper place on the stick so he can anticipate and execute the next musical effect.

Competency 16:	Be able to describe and perform the following bowings: Détaché, Staccato, Slurred Staccato, Martelé, Spiccato, Tremolo, Hooked Bowings, Louré, Sul ponticello, Col legno, Sul Tasto, Pizzicato.
Competency 16.1:	Détaché

Bowing Terms

Détaché

Literally, the term merely means detached notes that are not slurred. In practice it is the smooth change from one bow stroke to another. Often it is misrepresented as meaning strokes with a space between notes.

The détaché may be played at any part of the bow in a legato (smooth) manner. On the down-bow the second, third, and fourth fingers pull the bow, while on the up-bow the first finger pushes the bow. To achieve a smooth transfer in this finger action, the fingers of the right hand must be flexible and relaxed. An example of détaché bowing follows.

Activities

1. Practice each bowing on an open string as described in the paragraph that precedes it.
2. Practice the exercise.
3. Teach the bowing to another student.

Détaché

Wohlfahrt, Op. 45, No. 2

Self-Check List

	Yes	No
a. Do you feel the transfer of "push" and "pull" with the fingers as described in the opening paragraph?	☐	☐
b. Is the dynamic level (forte) the same at the frog, middle, and point?	☐	☐

Competency 16.2:   Staccato

Staccato

The staccato note is a short, stopped note played with the bow remaining on the string. There are many types of staccato; the style of music determines the type to be played.

Each stroke consists of a downward *press* followed by a *release*. The bow remains in constant contact with the string. A good rule to apply to the duration of a staccato note is that it is one-half of its written value (written ♩; played ♪𝄾). A musical example follows.

Staccato

Rodolphe Kreutzer

Self-Check List

	Yes	No
a. Do you get the press and release feeling in the first finger on the bow?	☐	☐
b. Is each eighth note of equal value in duration?	☐	☐

Competency 16.3:   **Slurred Staccato**

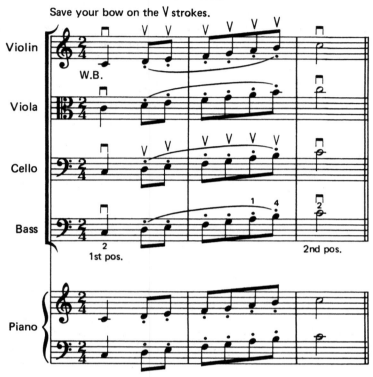

Self-Check List

	Yes	No
a. Do you have sufficient bow before reaching the last note of the slurred staccato?	☐	☐
b. Do you still feel the "bite and release" in the fingers of the right hand?	☐	☐

Competency 16.3.1:　Slur

Slur

Slurred notes are those that continue in the same direction or follow in sequence without a bow change. The character of slurred notes may vary. It may be smooth, staccato, or even spiccato. See the following examples.

Slur (Smooth)

1. Staccato (on the string)

2. Spiccato (V V V off the string)

Competency 16.4:   Martelé

Martelé

The martelé is a staccato stroke that is referred to as a "hammered" stroke. Each stroke must be prepared for by pressure before playing and followed by an immediate release of pressure. At the same time the bow is drawn quickly. The next stroke follows the same procedure—pressing, releasing, and at the same time moving the bow quickly. As in staccato, the bow remains in contact with the string at all times. However, martelé is more accented and it is marked with a wedge (∨). The martelé is usually played with the upper third of the bow, while the *grand martelé* is played with the whole bow. An example of the martelé stroke follows.

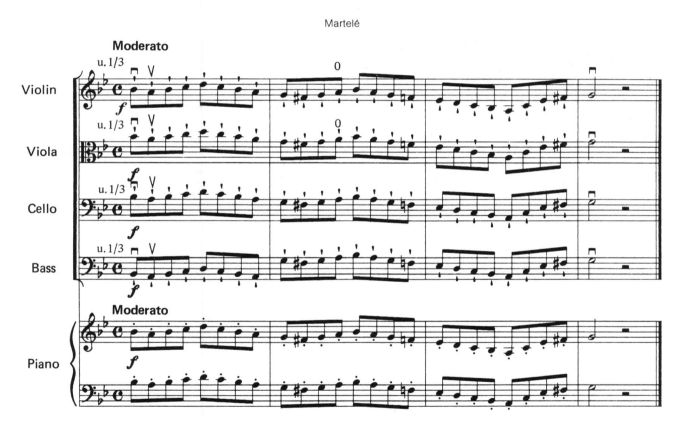

Self-Check List

	Yes	No
a. Does the bow remain at the upper third as you "hammer" each stroke?	☐	☐
b. Is the bow moving fast enough so that you are using the *entire* bow when playing #2, whole bow and still maintaining the "hammered" effect?	☐	☐

Competency 16.5:   Spiccato

Spiccato

The spiccato is an off-the-string bow stroke. It is sometimes referred to as "bouncing bow." However, one must be careful not to assume that the bow is bounced like a ball. Actually, the spiccato bow moves in a horizontal direction like a détaché bow except that there is a lift before and after the stroke, creating the bouncing effect. Occasionally, one uses a pure vertical motion for special effects.

There are two broad categories of spiccato notes, controlled and uncontrolled. On controlled strokes the right arm is primarily responsible for the style. On uncontrolled strokes, such as *sautillé* or *ricochet*, the execution is a result of the natural tension and spring of the bow. The right arm is completely relaxed for all forms of spiccato bowings.

A beginning student should experiment to find which part of the bow is most resilient; this is the section that gives the stick its best springing effect. Examples of spiccato bowing follow.

Spiccato

Menuetto   Joseph Haydn

Self-Check List

	Yes	No
a. Is the bow moving in the same direction that one uses for the detaché stroke and *not* up and down like a bouncing ball?	☐	☐
b. Does your right arm feel relaxed and not tense as you play the stroke?	☐	☐

Competency 16.6:   Tremolo

Tremolo

The term "tremolo" signifies the technique of moving the bow as rapidly as possible back and forth for the duration of the note value. It is best achieved at the point of the bow with a rather straight arm, but not rigid. To achieve the necessary speed of the stroke, primarily use the fingers and hand from the wrist. It may be played anywhere on the string—near the bridge, over the fingerboard, etc. Here is a musical example.

Tremolo

César Franck

Self-Check List

	Yes	No
a. Is the right arm rigid while the wrist moves flexibly back and forth?	☐	☐
b. Is the bow staying at the point?	☐	☐
c. Are you making a crescendo by expanding the area being covered at the upper half of the bow?	☐	☐

Competency 16.7:   Hooked or linked bowings

Hooked bowing

The term hooked bowing is applied to the technique of tying or slurring notes to avoid awkward bowings or improper accents. An example follows.

Hooked Bowing

Hector Berlioz

Self-Check List

	Yes	No
a. Does your bow move in a straight line and stay in the same spot on the string when playing a hooked bowing? (It should not be sliding up on the fingerboard or down against the bridge)	☐	☐

Competency 16.8:   Louré

Louré (portato)

The louré or portato style is a semistaccato type of bowing that is smoothly separated, or "pulsed." It is used to enunciate certain notes without pausing between them. To accomplish this type of bowing, a slight pressure is placed on the notes, as indicated in the musical example that follows.

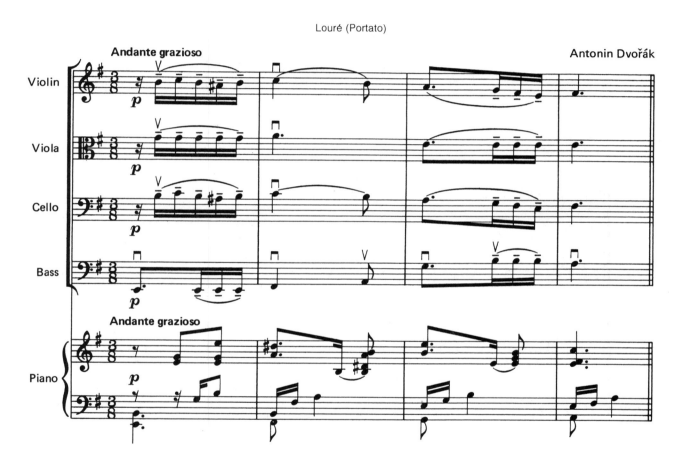

Louré (Portato)

Antonin Dvořák

Self-Check List

	Yes	No
a. When making the separations in the above exercise, does it sound smooth and not staccato in character?	☐	☐

Competency 16.9:   Sul ponticello

Sul ponticello

This type of bowing is done with the hair of the bow as close to the bridge as possible. To acquire the desired effect, it is helpful to tilt the bow hair slightly away from the bridge. See the musical example that follows.

Sul ponticello (German: "am Steg")

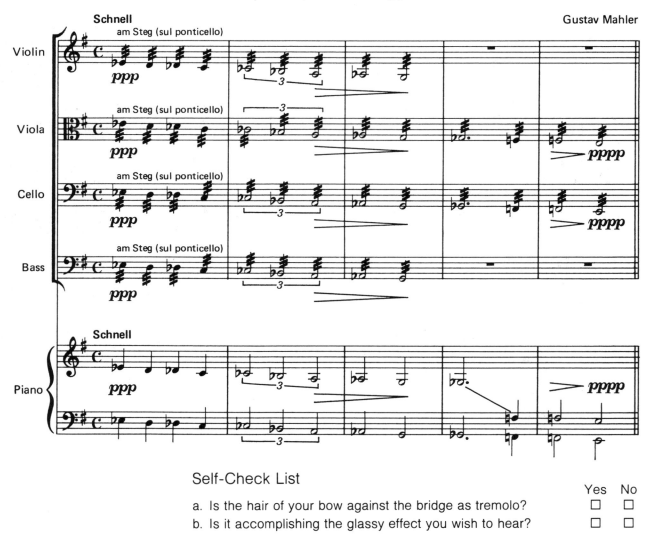

Self-Check List

	Yes	No
a. Is the hair of your bow against the bridge as tremolo?	☐	☐
b. Is it accomplishing the glassy effect you wish to hear?	☐	☐

Competency 16.10:   Col legno

Col legno

Literally the term means "with the wood." In performing this type of bowing, the string is struck (or tapped) with the wood side of the bow. It is helpful to tilt the bow so that the hair is turned away from the bridge. Col-legno style is generally performed with the upper half of the stick. A musical example using this technique follows.

America the Beautiful

Samuel A. Ward

Self-Check List

	Yes	No
a. Practice moving and going from arco to col legno right-hand position silently. Can you do it comfortably?	☐	☐
b. Practice playing from arco to col legno on an open string. When you move to col legno is the bow hair turned away from the string?	☐	☐

Competency 16.11:   Sul tasto

Sul tasto

This style gives a "sotto-voce" effect. It is performed with the bow placed over the fingerboard. The fingers of the right hand should be completely relaxed and holding the bow rather loosely. See the musical example that follows.

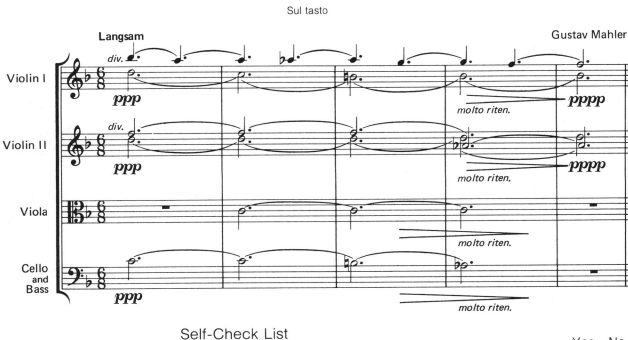

Sul tasto

Langsam   Gustav Mahler

Self-Check List

	Yes	No
a. Is the bow over the fingerboard when playing the above notes or on an open string?	☐	☐
b. Do the fingers of the right hand feel relaxed?	☐	☐

Competency 16.12:   Pizzicato

Pizzicato

Pizzicato means literally "to pluck." It may be done with the right hand, or with the left hand if the right hand is occupied with bowing. Modern music may require "nail" pizzicato, where the string is plucked with a fingernail; "snap" pizzicato, which is achieved by plucking the string with such force that it snaps against the fingerboard; "thumb" pizzicato, which is accomplished by softly stroking the string with the fleshy part of the thumb; or the two-fingered pizzicato, used for rapid passages and also used in avoiding an arpeggio effect.

Pizzicato

Peter Ilyich Tchaikovsky

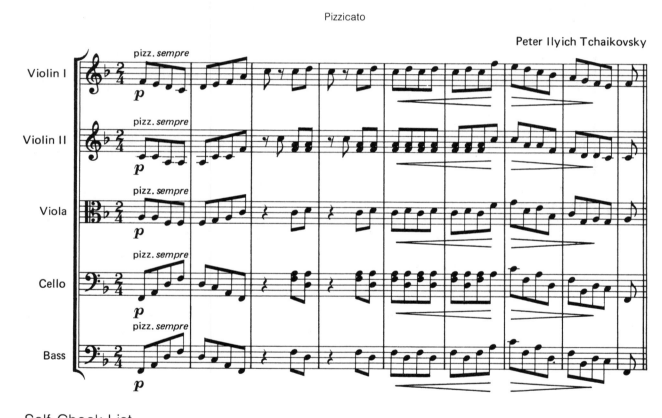

Self-Check List

	Yes	No
a. Is your thumb against the fingerboard? (Although not essential, this is desirable for security.)	☐	☐
b. Are you plucking over the fingerboard?	☐	☐

Competency 16.13:   Collé

Collé

This stroke begins with the bow being placed on the string similar to an V bow spiccato. At the moment of contact, the string is pinched lightly but with a sharp attack. As soon as the note is sounded, the bow is immediately lifted off the string in preparation for the next stroke. An example follows.

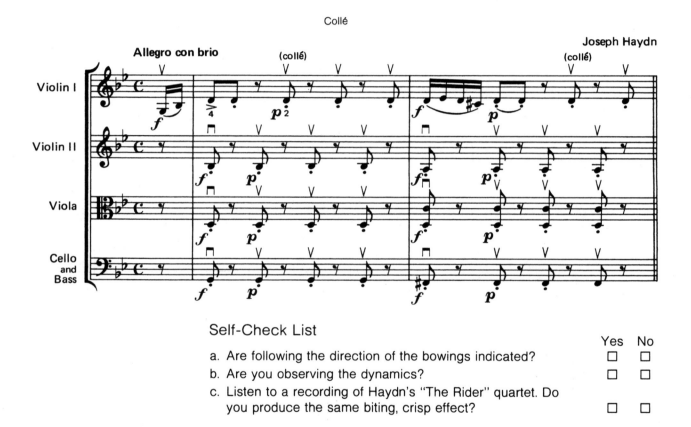

Collé

Joseph Haydn

Self-Check List

	Yes	No
a. Are following the direction of the bowings indicated?	☐	☐
b. Are you observing the dynamics?	☐	☐
c. Listen to a recording of Haydn's "The Rider" quartet. Do you produce the same biting, crisp effect?	☐	☐

Competency 16.14:   Scordatura Tuning

Scordatura

A special scheme to tune the open strings in such a way that unusual effects, such as tone clusters, can be created by merely playing open strings. It literally means to retune the strings to pitches other than the established pitches and can be used in a variety of ways.

To Robert Klotman
O He Did Whistle and She Did Sing
(carol for children's voices in unison and two violins and cello, open strings)
by Richard Felciano

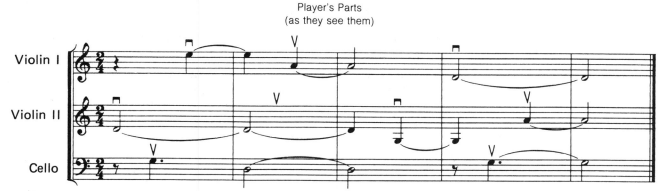

Player's Parts
(as they see them)

Activity and Check List

1. Create a composition for the class using scordatura tuning

Self-Check List

	Yes	No
a. Did the composition have melodic, harmonic, and rhythmic interest?	☐	☐

Competency 17:   Be able to mark bowings in a string part.

Some Basic Bowing Guidelines

One must remember that none of these rules is binding. There are many exceptions that are dictated by musical concerns and one can find instances where two outstanding string teachers will disagree over the same passage. These rules are merely set up to establish guidelines for the inexperienced string teacher.

1. Measures usually begin with a down-bow.
2. To comply with rule number 1, notes that begin before a bar line, if they consist of an odd number of separate bows, begin with an up-bow.

3. A dotted eighth and sixteenth are usually linked. (See hooked bowing, p. 170).
4. If there are a succession of uninterrupted sixteenth notes without slurs, then each group of four begins with a down-bow.

5. To achieve a crescendo, it is better to move from the point to the frog. (An excellent example of an exception to rule number 1, employing rule number 5, is the Bach "Air on the G string," which begins with crescendo on a sustained whole note. It is better to begin with an up-bow.

6. Where long, sustained notes caused by ties, slurs, or tempo occur, it is better in orchestral playing to permit change of bow by different players at different times. One suggestion is: Do not change on a beat, and assign inside and outside players on each stand different desegnated times.
7. In syncopation, especially in accented or forte passages, the syncopated note is played with a down-bow.

8. When there is a tie or slur over a bar line, it is usually played with a down-bow.

Activities and Check List

1. To see how well you can apply the above rules, mark the bowings in the exercise below.
2. Mark the rule number in the exercise below.

Overture

Moderato   Handel/Klotman

Self-Check List

	Yes	No
a. Mark your score with the answers on page 180. Did you get them all correct?	☐	☐

Overture

Developing Concepts to Accommodate Basic Orchestral Bowing Problems and Learning to Use Double Stops

Common Orchestral Bowing Problems

Problems in orchestral bowing may be divided into two main areas: (1) subdividing the bow length for proper phrasing, and (2) planning the bow stroke so that a certain dynamic or a special bowing effect may be achieved. This does not mean to ignore specific technical bowings such as spiccato, staccato, etc.; all of these skills require the development of certain techniques that are important in the second category above. However, if an orchestra director is prepared to handle both of the main problems, then all that remains is for the players to acquire the skills needed to execute the specific effect, although this involves complications such as bow speed, relationship of the bow to the bridge, and bow pressure.

Faults commonly found in the execution of bowing style are (1) too high a bounce or too much bow used for the various bouncing effects, (2) too little bow used for the martelé or the marcato styles, (3) general failure to relax the bow arm, and (4) playing entirely on the extreme edge of the bow hair.

In a performance, the main considerations for music interpretation are period, style, and musical effects. Both director and players need a knowledge of bowing techniques, so that together they can produce a musical experience of value.

Double Stops

Double stops were introduced early in the study material as a technical device to accomplish the necessary "pull" and "push" for a full sound. In addition, double stops help develop correct ideas about the various right-arm levels and angles as one plays on the different strings.

Frequently when playing double stops a poor tone is produced because the bow is not resting evenly on both strings. When this happens, the student is usually playing with more pressure on one string than on the other. (The double bass rarely uses double stops, but, even so, it is helpful for the bass player to practice these exercises, since they contribute to an understanding of correct bowing angles. See Figure 10–1.)

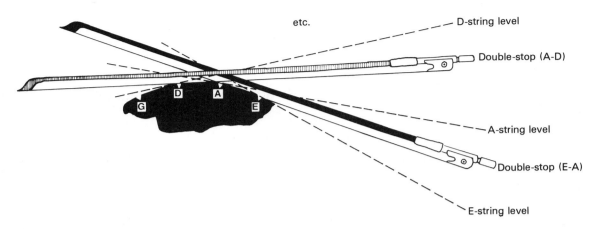

Figure 10-1

Learning to use double stops increases pitch perception. Intonation in orchestral playing is decidedly dependent on relative pitch, and double stops serve as a fine medium for ear training. However, in actual orchestral performance the particular string section is usually divided so that one group plays the top note, or group of notes, while the remaining instruments play the bottom note or notes (divisi).

The following musical diagram illustrates the use of double stops. (The violin strings are used to illustrate the principle. However, it applies to all string instruments.)

> Competency 18:   Be able to play double stops using combinations of fingers.

Double Stops Using Combinations of Fingers

Activities and Check List
1. Practice the following exercise

Self-Check List

	Yes	No
a. When playing double stops, do you hear both notes in equal strength?	☐	☐

Double Stops

1. "Fingers on Top"

Note: The fingers are reversed for the string bass.

2. "Fingers on the Bottom"

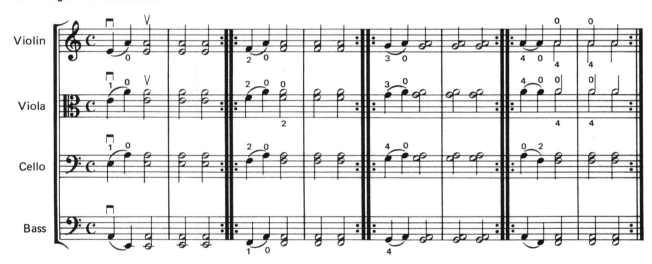

3. Thirds and Sixths

> Competency 18.1:   Be able to play double stops using additional combinations of fingers.

Occasionally it is necessary to play three- and four-note chords. These may be played in various ways, but generally as a two-note arpeggio beginning with the bottom notes, followed by a double stop using the top two notes. As the student progresses, he will discover other ways of executing double stops; however, until he becomes proficient, he should follow the approach given below.

The following musical examples illustrate ways of playing of three- and four-note chords.

4. Chords on Three Strings

Three-note chords may be played in two ways:

1. As a broken arpeggio:

2. Martelé:

Press the bow firmly on the middle string at the frog and try to play simultaneously on all three strings.

Activities and Check List

1. Practice the following exercises.

Self-Check List

		Yes	No
a.	When playing the chord, do you hear all of the notes in equal strength?	☐	☐

Competency 18.2:   Arpeggios

Arpeggios

The arpeggio is nothing more than a broken chord. The technique for arpeggios is similar to the one used with double stops, except that each note is played individually in the specified rhythm. (See the following musical examples.)

Arpeggios

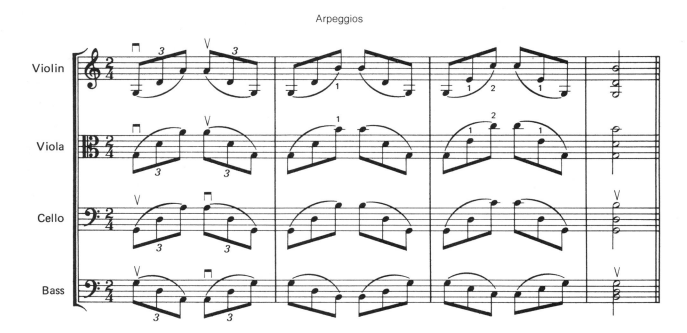

5. Chords Using Three and Four Strings

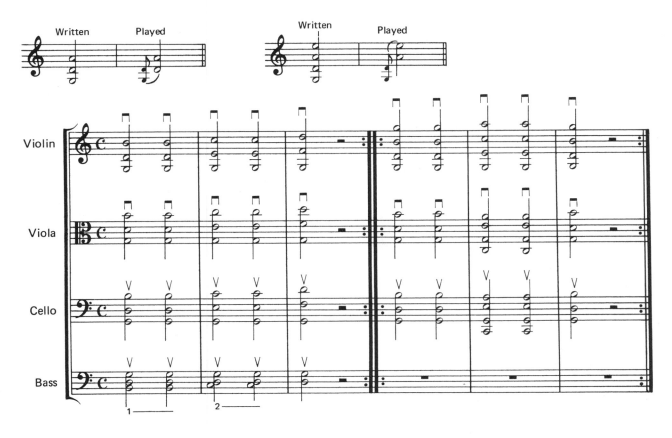

Self-Check List

	Yes	No
a. When playing the chords, do you hear all of the notes in equal strength?	☐	☐
b. Are the intervals in tune or are you merely putting fingers down?	☐	☐

Part V
Advanced Class Instruction

Explaining and Demonstrating Shifting into Five Positions

Competency 19:	Be able to perform exercises in the first five positions for each of the string instruments.

Position Études

The usefulness of the material in this chapter will depend on the achievement level of the class. If the students are not sufficiently advanced for position studies, this chapter may be omitted or postponed for use at a later time.

As a violin or viola player progresses into the higher positions, he moves his left thumb and elbow under the neck of the instrument. The hand actually begins to follow the contour of the instrument when the performer goes beyond the fourth position.

The cello or bass player should keep the left elbow raised as he moves to positions above the fourth position.

As the distance between the bridge and the left hand is shortened, that is, in the higher positions, the bow must be drawn proportionately closer to the bridge on all string instruments.

Although this text presents the positions in numerical sequence in order to acquaint the college student with the fingerboard, in actual teaching it is better to use a classroom text (such as the Applebaum book for violin, The Hans Sitt or Sevcik books for viola, Sebastian Lee's *Methods For Cello* and Simandl's *New Method for the Double Bass* or *The Artist's Studio for Strings: Shifting Development Studies* by Drew, Spinosa, and Rusch, published by Kjos Music Co.) that takes into consideration the problems inherent in each of the instruments.

The Bornoff *Finger Patterns in Position* is a complete shifting book for hetrogeneous (all strings) classes. A violin student should begin position work in third or fifth position, where the instrument itself can be used to find the position. For the cello or bass it is better to begin with the fourth position, where the same principle will apply.

The music on the following pages provides practice in the various positions.

Competency 19.1:	Be able to perform exercises in the second position.

Position Études

1. Second Position

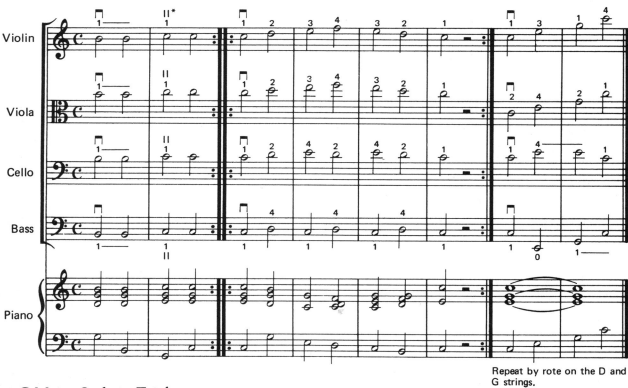

Repeat by rote on the D and G strings.

2. C Major Scale in Triplets

*Positions are indicated by Roman numerals in these studies.

3. "Lovely Evening" (Second Position)

Play first in unison (as written), then as a round.

Competency 19.2:   Be able to perform exercises in the third position.

4. Third position

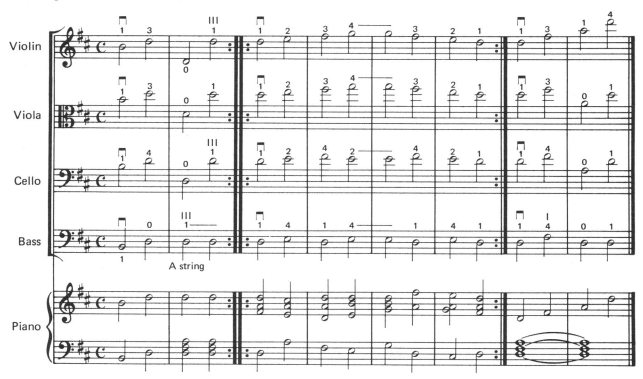

5. D Major Scale in Triplets

6. "Lovely Evening" (Third Position)

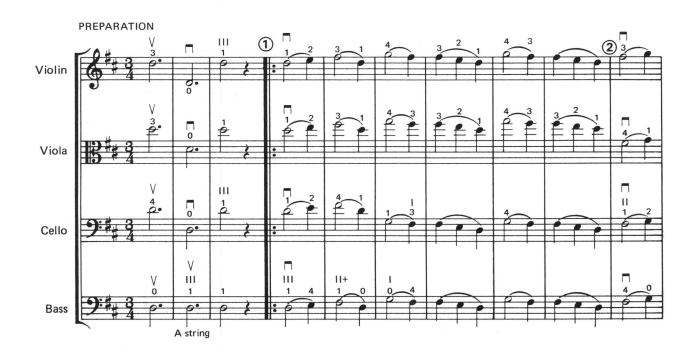

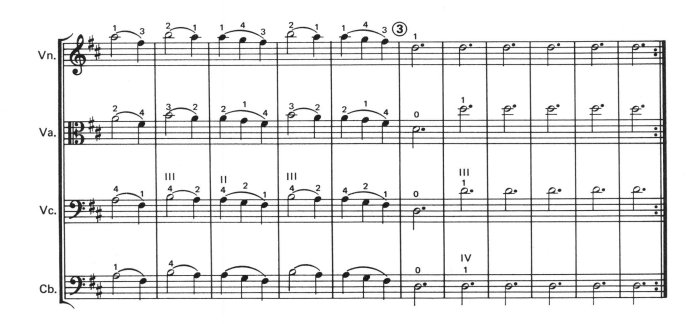

Shifting

The chief function of shifting is to extend the range of the instrument. There are seven basic positions, plus the variations added to accommodate modern fingerings; the string bass and cello also have intermediate (half) positions. For purposes of instruction, however, we will establish basic principles of shifting before exploring the fingerboard and its subdivisions.

Paul Rolland, a pioneer in analyzing movement in string playing, devised many exercises and organized these principles to promote freedom and mobility in shifting. Gerald Fischbach, in a series of articles for the *American String Teacher* (Summer/1980, Autumn/1980, Winter/1981), "Getting From There To Here with A Smile," outlined them as follows:

1. Shifting (and preshifting) activities should be introduced in the early lessons to encourage ease of movement and to avoid an artificial, learned fear of the upper region of the fingerboard.
2. Shifting activities should begin with large motions and refine to small.
3. At first, no specific pitch goals should be required. Progress gradually to specific points of departure and arrival.

To achieve a smooth shift, the left hand must be considered a unit that is free to move on the string. This freedom must be emphasized from the beginning of instruction.

One of the major obstacles to achieving a smooth shift is tenseness in the left thumb. To prevent this, it is helpful for the student to regard the thumb as an elevator that carries the hand when moving from a lower to a higher position.

The finger that is on the string when the student begins to shift remains on the string until the hand arrives in its new position. The finger that is to be used then falls into place, completing the shift. However, if the performer is moving to a new position, and the finger that is to be played is one lower than the finger initiating the shift, the finger that has a lower number falls into place while the shift is in progress.

All of the above motions must be practiced so that they can be accomplished with accuracy and in such a smooth manner that the various stages occur as though they were all part of one movement.

On backward shifts, the same rules of relaxation and freedom apply. However, it is the finger on the string that initiates the shift. Throughout, the basic relationship between the thumb and the fingers remains the same in the first four positions on cello and bass, and the first three positions on the violin and viola.

A second function of shifting is for "expressive" playing. This involves the "portamento," which in effect is a slight slide from one pitch to another. Since this can easily be overdone, it must be employed in a tasteful manner.

In the higher-numbered positions, the spacing between fingers is smaller.

In the third position on the violin and viola, it is advisable, for accuracy, to have the left wrist bend toward the body of the instrument so that the heel of the hand touches the body of the instrument.

The musical examples that follow are exercises for gaining proficiency in shifting.

Activities and Check List

1. Select a simple song from a songbook and perform it in a variety of positions, utilizing concepts of shifting learned in this unit.

Self-Check List

	Yes	No
a. Does the left hand move freely when shifting?	☐	☐
b. Are you able to move from one position to another comfortably?	☐	☐

Competency 20:	Be able to explain and demonstrate principles of shifting.

Exercises for Shifting

1. Moving Between First and Third Positions (Same Finger)

Note 1: Each shift is preceded by an interval in the first position to establish the proper interval and pitch relationships.
Note 2: When making the shifts, glide on the finger that is down.

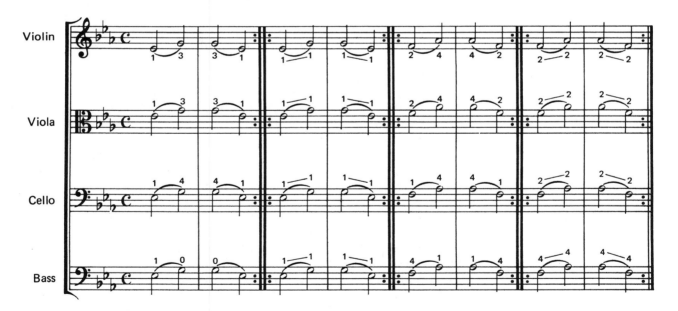

2. Moving Between First and Third Positions (Different Fingers)

Note: (♪) indicates approximately the pitch where the shift ends.

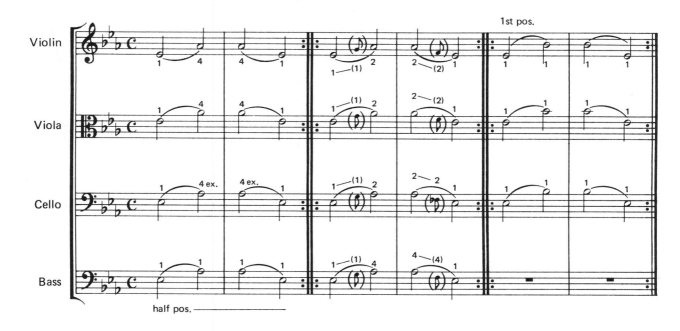

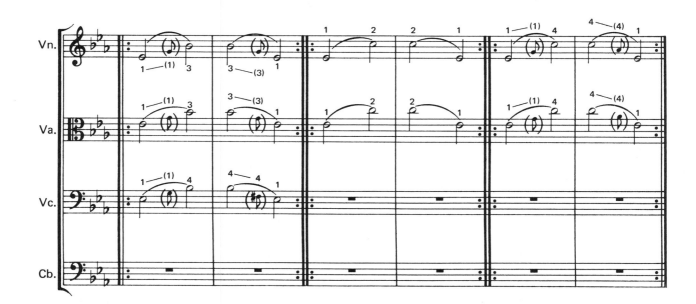

a. Repeat in $\frac{2}{2}$ (¢) time.
b. Follow the same procedure on the A string.

3. Étude in the First Three Positions
   a Slowly, with a separate bow for each note
   b As written (C)
   c Gradually increase speed to ¢

Hans Sitt (Adapted)

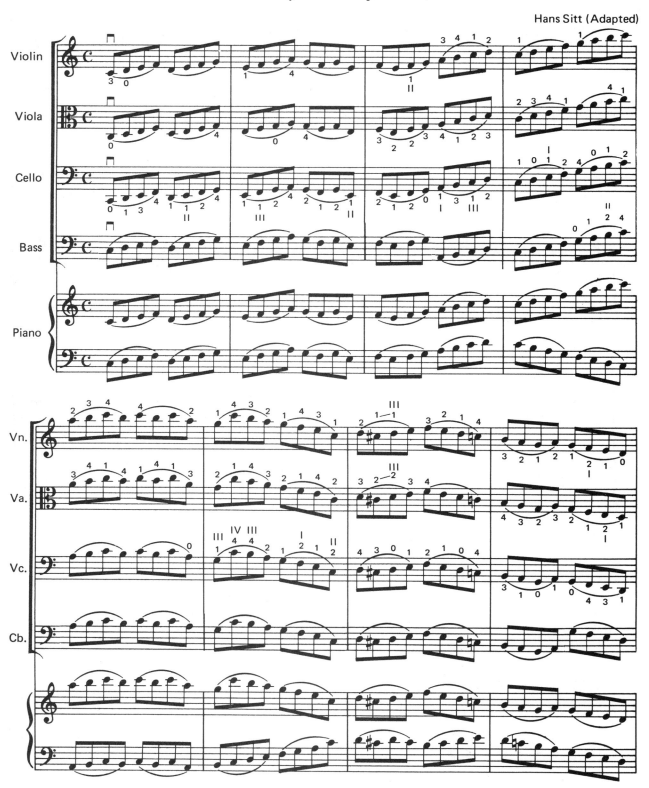

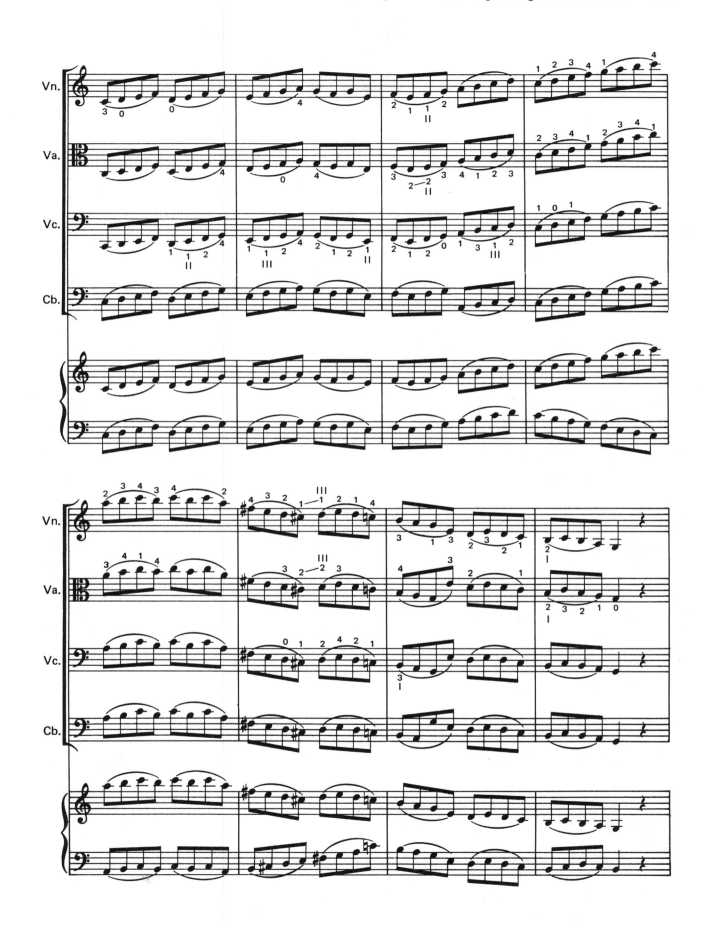

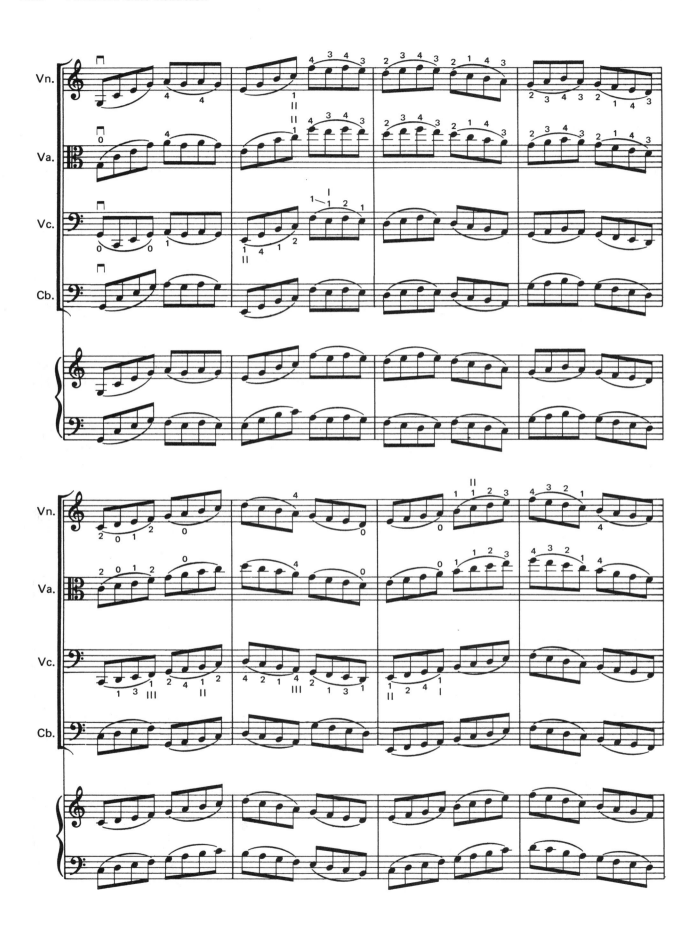

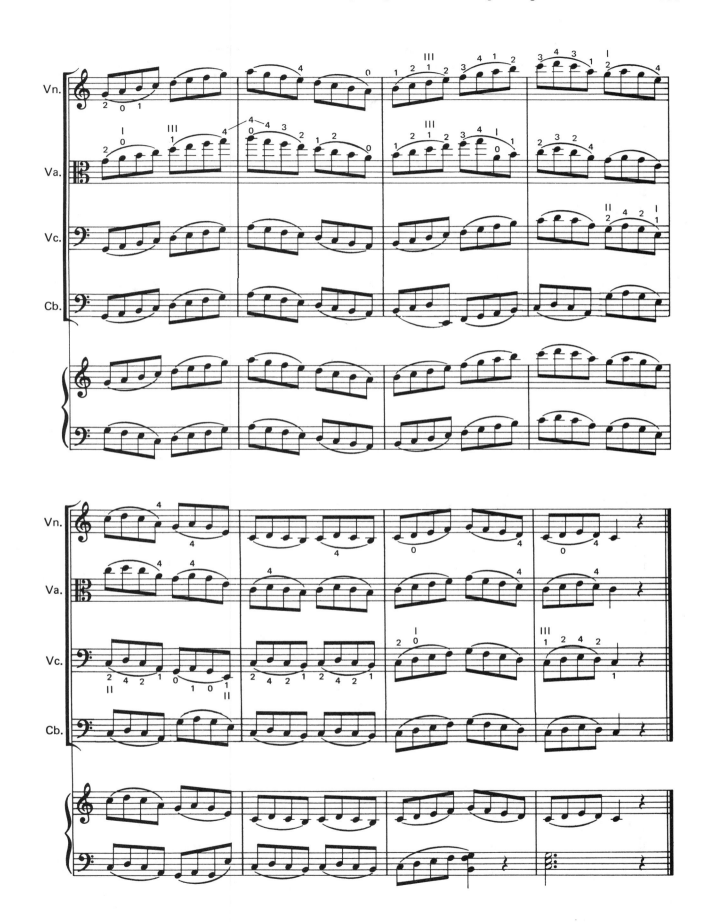

Competency 21:   Be able to perform exercises in the fourth position.

4. Fourth Position

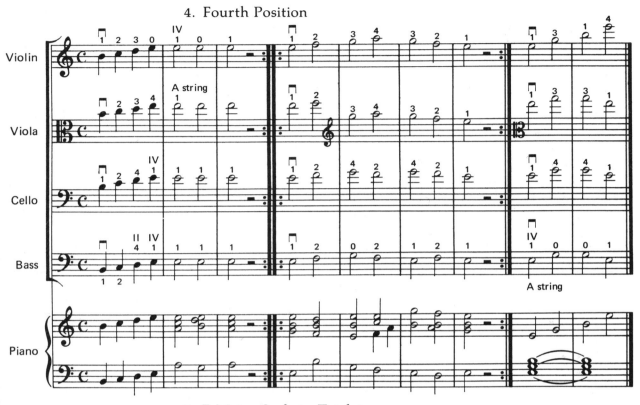

5. E Major Scale in Triplets

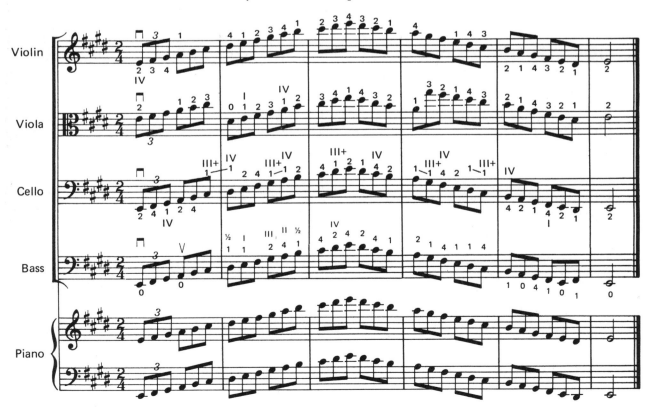

6. "Lovely Evening" (Fourth Position)

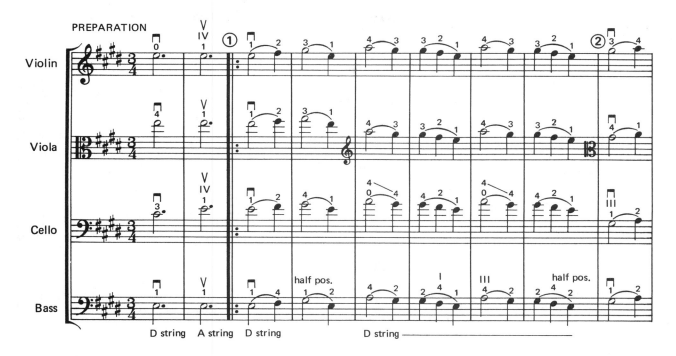

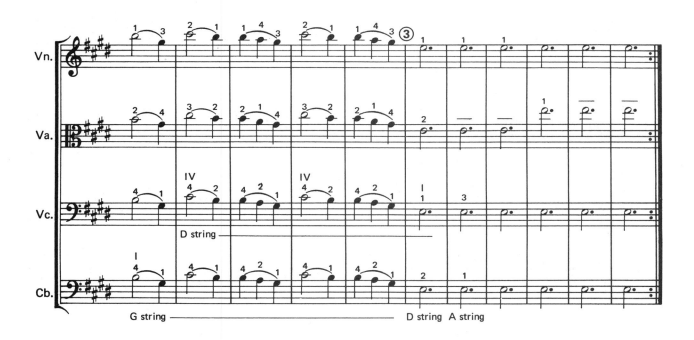

Competency 22:   Be able to perform exercises in the fifth position.

7. Fifth Position

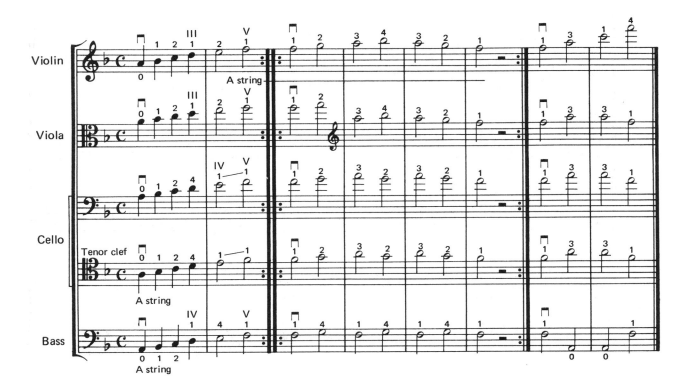

8. F Major Scale in Triplets

9. Shifting Études

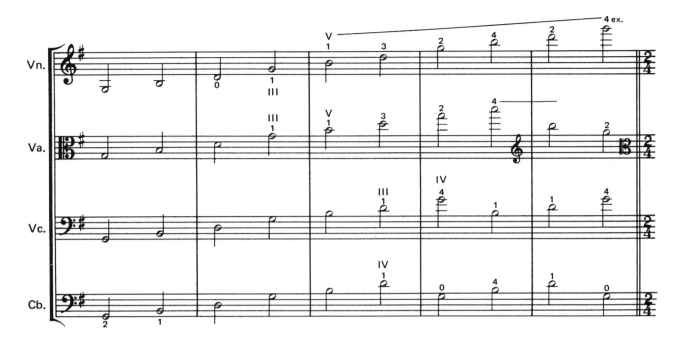

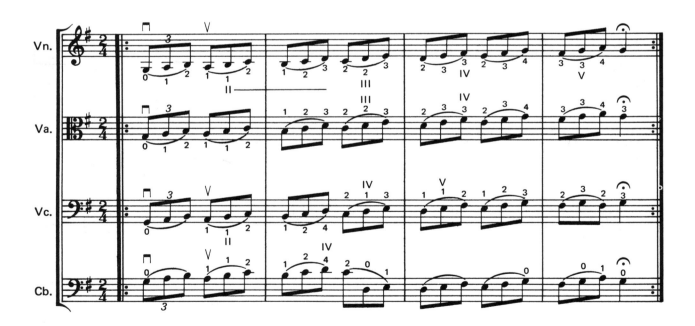

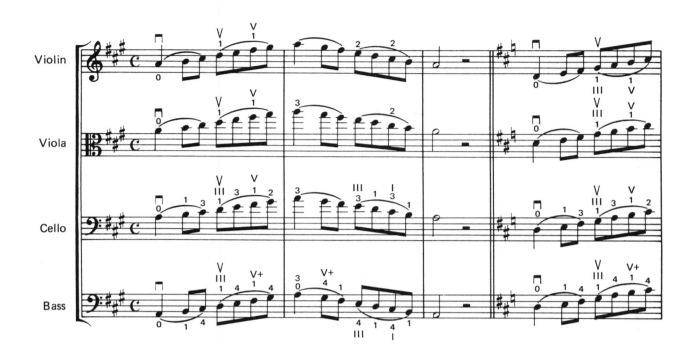

Legend
(Ensemble Study in Shifts and Positions)

Activities and Check List

1. Select a simple song from a songbook and perform it in a variety of positions, utilizing concepts of shifting learned in this unit.

Self-Check List

	Yes	No
a. Does the left hand move freely when shifting?	☐	☐
b. Are you able to move from one position to another comfortably?	☐	☐

Teaching the Vibrato

Competency 23:	Be able to explain and teach principles of vibrato on each of the instruments.

Another function of the left hand is to produce the vibrato. Many students are found to have a natural vibrato and they should be encouraged to experiment with it. However, some students, for a variety of reasons, find the vibrato difficult; placing undue pressure on them to vibrate too early in their development can be an inhibiting factor.

A smooth vibrato is continuous from tone to tone. Although a vibrato can vary in speed and intensity for musical effects, it must be even and consistent at all times, according to the type being utilized. Vibrato may be divided into three categories: (1) arm or forearm vibrato, (2) wrist vibrato, and (3) finger vibrato. The ideal vibrato utilizes elements of all three. It is important to avoid a tense, nervous vibrato that tends to stiffen the hand whenever it is used. Careful listening can best determine whether or not a student is producing a satisfactory vibrato.

Teaching the vibrato. Many students acquire a vibrato by instinct. For those who need to be taught, there are many techniques that assist in the process.

For violin or viola, one technique is to rest the instrument against a wall (see Fig. 12–1), and, with the left hand braced in the third position, practice oscillating movements from the wrist using eighth notes, triplets, sixteenths, and thirty-second notes. Do this with each of the four fingers on various strings. When

Figure 12-1

this exercise has been completed, move the hand to the first position and practice the same rhythmic patterns, but adding the forearm to the movement. The combination of forearm and wrist gives the basic vibrato utilized by most performers.

The cello or bass player may practice the same *rhythmic* exercises for vibrato with a shaking back-and-forth movement. Because of the angle of the instrument, there is more of a shaking arm movement, with wrist and arm operating as a single unit, rather than an oscillating movement as utilized by the violin and viola.

Under all circumstances the finger remains fixed; it should not slip or slide. However, this is not to say that the rhythmic impulses do not project through the finger; it is in fact, this projection of rhythmic impulses that creates the vibrato effect. It is fundamental to understand that all vibrato begins where the fleshy part of the fingertip meets the string. The larger muscles of the wrist and arm then follow in motion.

When a student has difficulty acquiring the "feel" of a vibrato, it is helpful for the teacher to physically assist the hand with the rocking motion (see Fig. 12–2). Some violin and viola students are helped by going through the process with the instrument in an under-the-arm position and sliding the left hand back and forth as if they were polishing the string gradually reducing the area until the finger becomes fixed on a note. The function of this sliding motion, back and forth, is to create the sensation or feeling of the vibrato movement.

Figure 12–2

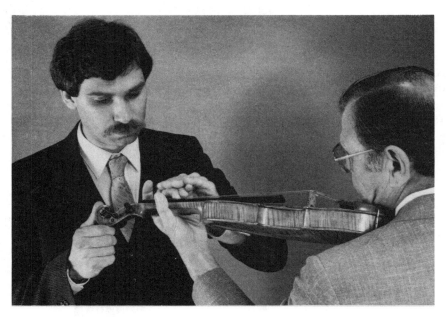

Difficulties in producing a relaxed, even vibrato are usually caused by tension in the left hand that may result from the student either squeezing the thumb against the neck or gripping the instrument with the left hand rather than holding it with the

Figure 12-3

jaw in the chin rest. To achieve a desirable vibrato the left hand must be limp and the fingers flexible.

The cello and bass vibrato is achieved by having the forearm and hand, from the elbow to the finger tip, roll back and forth in a wide arc. This rolling movement should be even and with as little effort and is possible. (See Fig. 12–3.)

Musical exercises to provide practice in vibrato follow.

Activities and Check List

1. Practice the vibrato etudes that follow in the third position on all four strings, varying the rhythm as indicated below the exercise.
2. Practice the same exercise in the first position on all four strings varying the rhythm as indicated below the exercise.

Vibrato Studies

Note 1: The ear discerns the highest pitch reached during the vibrato. To sound in tune, the vibrato must roll from the exact pitch to a pitch slightly below it and then back.

Pitch

Note 2: Be certain that the thumb of the left hand is free of the neck of the instrument.

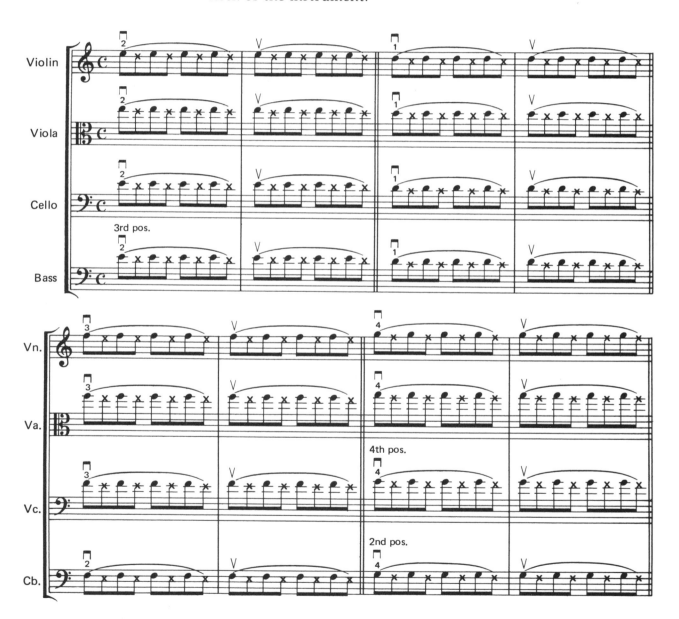

a. Do these exercises on all strings.
b. Do the same exercises in the first position.
c. Vary the rhythm:

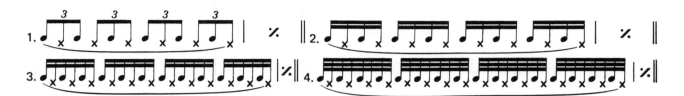

Self-Check List

	Yes	No
a. With each different rhythmic pattern does the vibrato sound even?	☐	☐
b. Can you vary the speed from vibrato at different times and still hear it sounding even?	☐	☐

Learning Unit 13

Teaching the Use of Harmonics

Competency 24:	Be able to play and explain natural harmonics.

In string playing, harmonics are divided into two categories, *natural* and *artificial,* and a single harmonic note may be produced in several ways in either of these categories. The effect of a particular harmonic note may be due to the use of a particular string, finger, or place on the string. Each method produces a different tone coloring; composers, writers, and conductors usually designate the method best suited to the effect they are trying to produce.

The tone produced when the bow is drawn across an open string is called the *fundamental.* The pitch of the fundamental is determined by the *nodes,* which are the stationary points at either end of the vibrating string; in the case of an open string, the nodes are the nut and the bridge. By touching an open string at the midpoint *lightly,* so that it is not pressed against the fingerboard, and drawing the bow across the string, a natural harmonic is obtained one octave above the fundamental.

Pressing a finger down *firmly* at the midpoint of the string introduces a new nodal point—the point of contact between the string and the fingerboard. Since the location of the nodes determines the fundamental, a new fundamental is produced. If one maintains this new nodal point with the first finger and touches the same string lightly at a different point with the third or fourth finger, the result, when the bow is drawn across the string, will be an artificial harmonic. Artificial harmonics may be produced by touching the string lightly at points one-third, one-quarter, or one-fifth of the way along the effective part of the string (i.e., the part bounded by the bridge and the nodal point maintained by the first finger).

When playing harmonics, it is a good idea to move the bow closer to the bridge than usual and apply the usual amount of pressure. There is a tendency on the part of inexperienced players to relax the pressure of the bow arm because they are touching lightly with the fingers of the left hand.

Harmonics may be introduced early in string instruction as a device to develop a good "pull" and correct use of the bow arm. Much will depend on the ability of the student and the teacher's background in proceeding at this level of instruction.

To indicate a natural harmonic, a composer writes the pitch at which the string is touched lightly and places a small circle above it; or else he indicates the place where the string is touched lightly by a diamond-shaped note. To indicate an artificial harmonic, a composer writes in the customary way the pitch at which the string is pressed firmly, and above it he writes a diamond-shaped note to indicate where the string is touched lightly.

The following musical examples illustrate the use of harmonics.

Activities and Check List

1. Play the examples of natural harmonics that follow:

Natural Harmonics

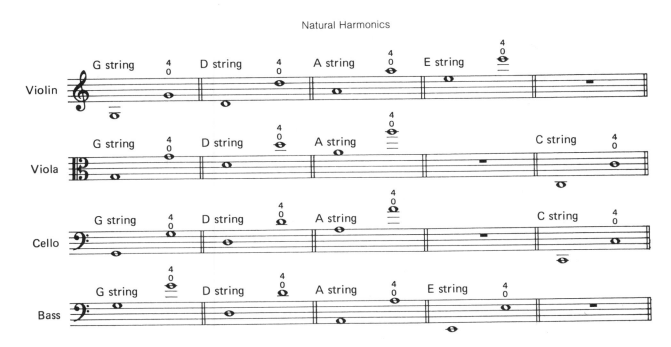

Individual Sections

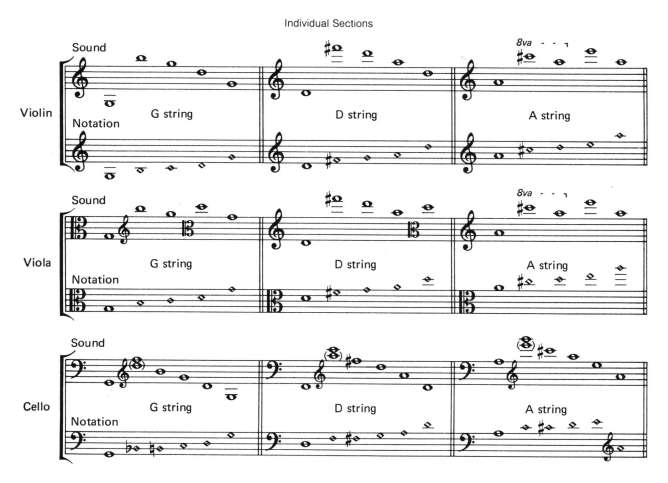

Note: On the cello and bass, for the natural harmonics in first position, one can get different notes a third apart depending on whether one plays the note high or low.

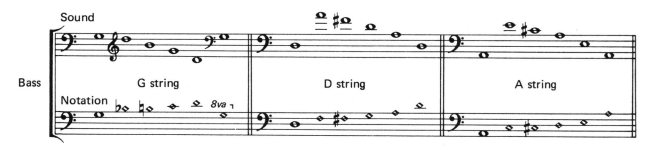

Competency 24.1:	Be able to play and explain artificial harmonics.

Activities and Check List

1. Play the artificial harmonics that follow:

Artificial Harmonics on D String
Individual Sections

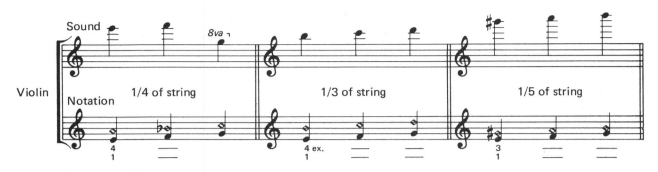

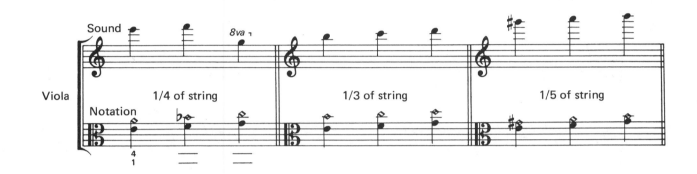

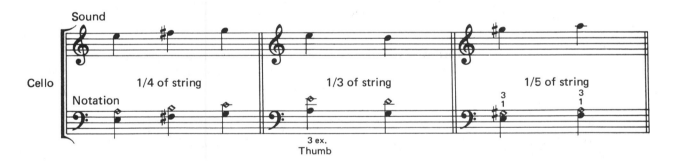

Artificial harmonics are not practical for the string bass in the lower positions because of the string length.

Self-Check List

	Yes	No
a. When playing the natural harmonics, do you maintain a full tone rather than a weak, squeaking sound?	☐	☐

Part VI

Developing String Programs in Schools

Creating Interest in Strings: Recruiting

A major responsibility of the string teacher is the task of bringing the joy of music making, and especially the thrill of playing a string instrument, to young people. Unfortunately, some teachers of strings approach this matter in the spirit of inducing pupils to take up the study of a string instrument principally for the purpose of building a school orchestra. The only valid purpose in creating interest in playing a string instrument should be, first of all, the musical growth and the musical pleasure of the pupils. If this is the genuine goal of the string program, there will be an orchestra—and a good one.

There are numerous ways of recruiting string players. Some of the most prevalent methods are described below and appraised from both positive and negative viewpoints.

The announcement method. This consists of making announcements, both in classrooms and in assemblies, to the effect that pupils may join the string program. Classroom teachers are asked to "talk it up." Parents are usually notified by mail, or else a printed announcement is sent home with the pupils. For creating interest in strings, this is probably the *least* effective and the least dependable means.

The lecture method. A typical example of this approach is for the teacher to appear before the students with a violin or a set of string instruments. He tells something of the history of the instruments; how they are constructed; the materials of which they are made, etc. The demonstration is usually concluded with an explanation of the personal rewards of playing an instrument, and other such benefits. Pupils may find this demonstration "interesting," but as an agency for recruitment it is usually not as effective as some of the other methods.

The guest artist performer. In an effort to arouse interest in playing a string instrument, some teachers who play well might perform before a class or student assembly, with the hope that the students will be inspired to the point of wanting to join the string program. Teachers who do not play so well themselves often bring in an outstanding performer for this purpose. This type of approach usually provides musical "entertainment" of a high order, but normally it induces only a few students to take up the study of string instruments. Perhaps the reason for this is the fact that even young people realize that to perform at such a high level of artistry requires unusual talent, plus many years of study and practice. Human beings are more inclined to want for themselves the things that they can accomplish and enjoy in a relatively short time.

The testing program.   Many schools rely on a testing program. The tests are not intended to eliminate students but to offer a means of communicating with the students and their parents. Once the tests are completed, letters are sent home requesting a conference or inviting parents to a demonstration concert or meeting. The letters usually state the purpose and objectives of the school music program and how strings contribute to it; they may contain information on how the child will benefit from playing. Although the testing plan has met with some success, it can be misleading in that it may misrepresent the student's talent. Tests containing little or no data on reliability and validity have limited values.

The string performance unit.   A more desirable plan is to present an instrument unit on instruments of the orchestra to the third- or fourth-grade music class. After a short introductory period, students have the opportunity to actually experiment with all of the string instruments. Those students who show interest are considered as potential string students. The plan has met with some success where sufficient time and/or money is allotted to the general music program; however, that is rarely the case.

The student string ensemble.   One of the more prevalent approaches used to create interest in strings is to select a group of students from the existing string program in the school, or from another school, and have them play for the music class. If this approach is used, it is a good idea to choose student performers whose ages approach the ages of the student audience. However, it is even better to have two performing groups: one group that is experienced and is somewhat advanced, and a second group that has had only a year or so of experience. The idea is that students in the audience are likely to feel that they, too, can do this.

The participation method.   This is by far the most effective means of creating interest in playing a string instrument. The children are given a quick, five-minute lesson on finding the open strings, and then they actually play the instruments while the orchestra or piano plays melody and accompaniment. The children get the feeling that they are playing, and they love it.

There is no substitute for personal participation in an activity. This is true in all life situations. For example, boys and girls might enjoy watching other boys and girls play some sport, but only in a passive or semipassive way. The real thrill comes from the experience of trying it oneself—even if one's efforts do not conform to all of the niceties of refined techniques. To become personally involved in something, whether or not by design, is to come closer to it. In using the participation method, the authors have observed many occasions where people—both young and old—who thought they had a strong dislike for music suddenly experienced an entirely different attitude; they actually wanted to become active music makers. It is human nature to want to work hardest at the things that have personal value and satisfaction, and that instill an inner feeling of success, or at least suggest that success is attainable, even if it requires effort on the part of the individual.

The two short pieces that follow are good examples of music that can be used in the participation method.

In the final analysis, the most effective agent for the promotion of string playing is the music teacher himself. It is his honest enthusiasm and belief in the inherent value of his task that sustains the interest of the students. A good teacher maintains a kindly attitude toward his class. While he must insist on a high standard of performance, a music teacher should never be unkind or destructive. Students thrive on praise and recognition, and teachers should be generous with these if interest is to be maintained.

Flow Gently Sweet Afton

Arranged by Ernest E. Harris

Triumphal March from "Aida"

Giuseppe Verdi (arranged by Ernest E. Harris)

The Developmental String Program

String study programs should offer a well-organized, sequential series of experiences that promote interest and contribute toward the development of the individual player. They should give students a musical objective for increasing and refining their technical proficiency so that as their "performance ability" improves, so does their musical understanding and sensitivity.

Students should be made aware of study objectives from their earliest stages of instruction. These goals may be in terms of physical movement, performance, skill (bowing, etc.), or specific pieces of music in their repertoire. As they achieve these goals, they enjoy an awareness of their own progress and success. A useful technique to motivate pupils is to make special assignments to individuals as well as class assignments. A performance, whether in front of a class, a homeroom, or a parents' meeting, is always a good incentive to practice. It is also helpful to keep daily practice records. If checked conscientiously, they provide another form of commitment toward developing the skills required for successful string playing.

Concerts and public performances are almost always motivating. These may be unison solos, including pieces for students from every level of proficiency, or informal demonstrations. Ensemble playing, introduced in the early stages of instruction, should be nurtured and encouraged until it reaches the sophisticated level of actual chamber-music performance.

Selecting Students

In many schools the theory prevails that "only the best and most talented students should be selected for string players." This theory has worked to the detriment of school orchestras. It conveys the idea that strings exist on a unique plateau and only the elite should be chosen to play them.

It is only natural that teachers prefer to work with students who are relatively far along in their musical growth. There are, however, many examples of students who indicated little ability when "tested," but who developed at a rapid rate after being exposed to musical experiences.

Schools should provide a trial period that would let any child who exhibits genuine interest have an opportunity to experiment with several string instruments. Thus, over a period of several months, a teacher could observe the child's musical growth, his musical awareness, and the development of his auditory perception. Additional information could be obtained from the classroom teacher, who observes the child's musical behavior pattern daily.

Physical characteristics.   Strings are the one instrumental family in the orchestra that is completely adaptable in size to accommodate the physical growth and characteristics of each child. No other family of instruments provides such flexibility. To assure maximum success, this advantage should be utilized to its utmost. Even the preschool child has a choice of instruments down to a one-sixteenth-size violin.

When selecting string players, it is well to observe the spread and general flexibility of the palm and fingers of the left hand, the size of the fingers, and the arm length. Children with short, stubby fingers, or those with extremely slender fingers will have some difficulty. But it is not necessary to be unduly concerned about the little finger. With sufficient spread of the palm and proper use of the left elbow, a small fourth finger is not a serious handicap. Children with a larger palm spread and wider fingers may choose correspondingly larger instruments; however, for the most auspicious beginning, the students should have exhibited some interest in these larger instruments. Much will depend on the teacher's judicious guidance.

Measuring a student for size. Many methods are employed to measure a student for the correct size of instrument (see pp. 10–12). For the violin or viola, another procedure is suggested: Measure the student's left arm from his armpit to the tip of his middle finger; then use the chart given below.

Arm Length	Violin	Viola
Under 18 in.	One-quarter size or smaller	—
18–21 in.	Half size	—
21–24 in.	Three-quarter size	Junior
24 in. or over	Full size	Three-quarter size

The cello and bass size is determined by a combination of factors—the student's arm length and his height. The following chart gives a rough guide for proper size.

Arm Length	Height	Cello	Bass
Under 18 in.	50 in.	One-quarter size or smaller	—
18–20 in.	52 in.	Half size	—
20–22 in.	56 in.	Three-quarter size	Half size
22–24 in.	60 in.	Full size	Three-quarter size (This is a full size for school use)

There are some visual guidelines. For the cello, the instrument is too large if the student has to drop his right shoulder and body to play at the tip of the bow. When he is seated properly, the top part of the lower bouts should be about at knee height. The neck block should come up to the student's breastbone.

For the bass, the student should also be able to play at the tip of the bow without dropping his right shoulder, and the fingerboard nut should be about even with the student's left eye. The length of the end pin can be adjusted to the player's height. The left hand should be able to encompass a major second (one full tone on the scale) with the first to the fourth fingers on the strings.

When in doubt, it is better to recommend a smaller instrument rather than one that is too large.

It is not uncommon to find that the instrument selected by the size of the left hand may utilize a bow that is too long for the student's right hand. In this case, have the student hold the stick at the frog as though he or she were going to play, and then tip it so that it is parallel to the right arm. Mark the stick with a piece of tape at the point where it reaches the student's shoulder; this indicates the length of his or her full bow. To have the student play beyond this point would necessitate swinging the arm away from proper bowing paths and would result in poor habits. It is not necessary to get a different bow, although it is preferable. As the student grows, the point of his or her full bow will be extended until it reaches the full length of the stick. It is important that the student should not try to play beyond the marked point until able to do so.

Selecting Materials

There is no one "method" book that will answer all problems and automatically ensure success. A music teacher should carefully examine all the books available and select materials on the basis of his or her own basic approach to teaching strings. Nothing is more revealing of a teacher's attitude about strings and about music in general than the materials he or she selects. It is the teacher's choices that will determine, in a sense, the musical development of the students.

In establishing criteria for selecting music, a few pertinent questions may be used as guidelines: (1) Does the material contain sufficient music of quality to challenge the inherent musical needs of the children? (2) is there a proper skill sequence to promote technical as well as musical growth? Does it contain material such as scales, bowing studies, rhythmic studies, and interval exercises? (3) Does the material embody the essential, basic principles that affect technique? (4) Does it offer music attractive enough to sustain a student's interest and keep him or her working diligently? (5) Are there enough pictures to illustrate proper techniques? (6) Is the estimated rate of progress correct for the purpose? (7) If the music is to be performed in public, is it within the scope of the student's technical proficiency so that it may be prepared within a reasonable amount of rehearsal time? (8) Does the material or "method" promote proper attitudes toward music as an art form?

Music selected for school string groups should be carefully edited and arranged so that it preserves the general effect desired by the composer.

In addition, students should not be subjected only to skill studies. From the beginning every effort should be made to provide satisfying musical experiences. Enjoyment and perceivable progress are the essential ingredients for success. They should be the major considerations in the selection of all music.

Multiple-part Music

The opportunity to perform still seems to be the major incentive for practice. Unfortunately, students are all too often forced to perform music that is beyond their technical and musical ability. This not only inhibits proper instruction but contributes to improper playing habits and false standards.

Such a mistake is entirely unnecessary. Through multiple-part music, students can still have thrilling, satisfying experiences without being forced into premature solo performances. A music director planning a group performance may simplify any part that is beyond the technical range of a student's ability without destroying the musical effect. In addition, there are many compositions specially written for this type of performance. One example is Vaughan Williams' *Concerto Grosso for String Orchestra*, which even includes parts for an open-string orchestra. (The criteria for such music should be that the easy parts should be within the technical limitations of the less skilled players and that the overall sound should be substantially satisfying to the more mature performers.)

The Oberlin, Ohio, community has in past years held an effective string festival; it always featured a multiple-part composition that included beginning string classes, the string players of the high-school and college orchestras, and string players in the adult community.

Karl Kroeger has composed for the Eugene, Oregon, school system a *Prelude for Massed String Orchestras*, which is now available through the University Microfilms, Ann Arbor, Michigan. This composition employs beginning elementary, advanced elementary, junior-high-school, and high-school orchestras, offering valid motivation and encouragement for players of lesser ability. It also provides learning experiences that include living, practical examples of good tone quality, good posture, and proper performance habits. There is a tremendous potential in this type of music for the school orchestra.

Heterogeneous and Homogeneous String Classes

There is no real agreement on the merits of homogeneous versus heterogeneous string classes. In schools the choice is too often dictated by expediency and schedules.

A good formula might be that with the younger students (elementary), single-instrument classes are preferable. As students mature, they become more interested in the composite sound of the orchestra, and then the heterogeneous approach becomes the more favorable.

In secondary schools (junior and senior high schools), departmentalized schedules make it possible for a string class to meet daily. Here the students progress faster and are able to start playing simple ensemble music. In this situation the heterogeneous class provides greater flexibility, sustains interest, and offers a greater variety of literature and activities for instruction purposes.

On the other hand, the homogeneous class makes teaching easier. There is less concern with providing interesting activities for the violin players, for example, while working on a specific problem involving the bass players. In addition, among the various instruments there are several differences in hand position and technique that might be confusing if taught in a mixed class. (See "Common Errors," p. 34–40.) In the final analysis, the teacher must study his own situation and determine what is best for his type of program.

In both heterogeneous and homogeneous classes there are certain techniques for class teaching that should be utilized. Among these are the following: (1) Do not remain static. Circulate among the class and work with individuals at all times. (2) Devise a variety of activities that enable the individual to perform and still involve the entire class. For example, an individual plays—the group responds; class fingers the notes while an individual performs; student plays—the class analyzes; recital hours, etc. (3) Utilize a variety of bowings even in "unison" performance, to allow for individual difference, (some pizzicato, others arco; some using slurred bowings, others marcato; etc.).

The Second-Year String Class

The objectives of a second-year string class are (1) improving reading ability through ensemble experiences, (2) further developing the use of the bow arm, (3) introducing the use of positions, and (4) developing a vibrato. The challenge in a class situation is how to provide this instruction to individuals of varying abilities and still maintain full class activity throughout the period.

Since private study is the best solution for developing facility and tonal concepts on an instrument, and since the class supplies the best ensemble experience, it is best to combine some of the elements of the private studio with the socially motivating advantages of the classroom. Under these conditions, the materials used in a class would include études as well as ensemble music.

To implement this twofold plan, each student in a mixed-instrument class should have a separate étude book. Assignments are made to each group of players, and the students then spend half of the period in supervised unison practice and half in ensemble playing.

Thus the director may spend a part of each daily period teaching a homogeneous group in the classroom while the remaining students are assigned practice rooms. Individual lessons need not be given during the instruction period, but members of the group should receive help as it is needed. Études may be played in unison and rehearsed as if they were unison sections in a composition while the teacher circulates around the room making individual corrections. Individuals may be asked to play certain significant passages and, to keep everyone occupied, those who are not playing may finger the passage silently. The group may be asked to analyze an individual's performance. Some of the students may be asked to prepare études as solos and perform a short recital during the lesson period. Here again silent exercises may be utilized while an individual is playing.

Designating a variety of bowings will help to accommodate the differing rates of acquiring skills in a class. For example, one group may be reviewing an eighth-note étude with a détaché bowing, while another group that had performed the exercise satisfactorily the previous day could be playing the same étude with two slurs and two separate bows, that is,

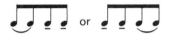

This manner of teaching not only provides for individual abilities, but begins to develop the second objective, which is expanded use of the bow arm.

During the period of homogeneous instruction, be certain that an aide, who may be a class chairman or an advanced student, is constantly supervising the students in the practice rooms. When the proper attitude has been established, students enjoy practicing in groups and helping each other. One student can take charge of the group while the director checks the practice rooms to see that all is going well. Instruction should take only part of a period; however, the remainder should be spent checking and evaluating assignments. All of these conditions help impel students to work.

Ensemble playing. Facility in reading music is best developed through ensemble playing. There is a good deal of easy ensemble or string-orchestra music available. Many of the heterogeneous-class methods have a second book that can be used as an easy orchestra folio. During the ensemble-playing segment of the instruction period, students learn to play under the direction of a baton, and there should be considerable emphasis on dynamics, balance, phrasing, ensemble relationships, and similar elements of ensemble playing.

Private instruction. Playing in the school orchestra is a special activity designed for students with special interests and abilities. Therefore it is justifiable to encourage students who qualify to play in the orchestra to study privately, especially when interest and talent warrant it. In addition, as better string-class instruction is offered during the early years, more students are motivated to study privately as a result of their musical growth in the class.

However, in the public schools, circumstances do not always permit private lessons. There may be financial restrictions, or some students may live where teachers are not available. It then becomes incumbent upon the school music teacher to provide instruction for these children in class.

Schools of String Teaching

Preschool Instruction: Suzuki Approach

In 1964, at a meeting of the Music Educators' National Conference in Philadelphia, Shinichi Suzuki presented some concepts regarding the musical education of preschool children in Japan that might well be called revolutionary. One of Suzuki's basic ideas was that educators had been underestimating the learning potential of small children. He also contended that environmental factors are far more important in the musical growth of a child than is so-called talent. Though the users of the present book may not be directly involved in preschool instruction, all teachers of string instruments should be informed and prepared to discuss the Suzuki method when they become involved in school music programs.

Dr. Suzuki's use of the word "environment" did not refer to a socioeconomic setting. What he suggested was a conditioning program based on a planned and supervised program of musical training at an early age. He proposed that any teacher can provide a stimulating musical environment based on an ear-conditioning program that utilizes musical examples that have proved to be motivating for children. On this premise, any child can play the violin just as he learns to speak his native tongue. Incidentally, this does not disregard the talent factor: the ultimate level that the child will achieve is determined by this factor.

Dr. Suzuki has pointed out that a child learns to speak his native or "mother" tongue through the natural method of imitating his mother and other members of the family, not by formal reading materials. By applying this principle to violin playing, he has proved that much of what we have assumed to be "inborn genius" actually has been developed by applying proper educational principles at an early age. Basic to his method is listening to high-quality performances on a recording or tape. It is his contention that music should be learned from listening before music reading. Each piece is memorized from listening to the tape or record for every lesson.

Another fundamental principle in this approach is the absolute mastery of each step before proceeding to the next. One should not measure progress by quantity or speed but rather by quality.

A significant feature of this program is the inclusion of interested parents and, as always, sensitive, enthusiastic, patient teachers. Through parental involvement, playing an instrument becomes a family affair—a joint exploration into the joys of making music. In addition, by attending the lesson the parent becomes more responsible for providing the necessary home environment and overseeing the practice period.

Lessons in the pure Suzuki schools are private although other students and parents are in attendance so that even a private lesson has an audience. Periodically teachers will get their students together at recitals, concerts, or conferences for "play-ins" where solo literature is performed "en mass." These programs are designed not only as an opportunity to culminate certain learning experiences at various levels, but also to inform parents and friends about the progress these children are making. A fundamental premise in the Suzuki philosophy is that a child should not discard a composition once it is learned. It is then that the musical, artistic learning really asserts itself. By frequent repetition the child refines each piece. It become review and reinforcement and these "play-ins" provide enjoyment and motivation for retaining these learned pieces.

In summary, the Suzuki approach is based on the following:

1. An organized sequence of musical materials that follow an order based on technical, musical levels of ability,
2. Recordings by leading artists that provide models for students to emulate,
3. Parents attending every lesson to assist in the learning process,
4. Games that use physical activity to free the body and remove tensions in playing, and
5. A philosophy expressed in the text, *Nurtured by Love*.

The Rolland Approach

Paul Rolland's approach was initially organized for the violin but as concepts were developed they were later applied to other string instruments. The central premise of his approach was that movement training, designed to release the student from excessive tensions could be presented from the incipient stages in an organized plan that would contribute to faster learning and better playing in all facets of instruction. His "action studies" culminated in a method book, *Prelude to String Playing*, published by Boosey & Hawkes and coauthored Ed Krolick, Bassist, and Margaret Rowell, cellist. A later supplement to the *Prelude* was *Read and Play*, which was essentially a rote to note approach and also published by Boosey & Hawkes. His visual materials and other text contributions may be secured through the Illinois String Research Project, c/o University of Illinois, Urbana, Illinois. ASTA has published *The Writings of Paul Rolland: An Annotated Bibliography* by Mark Joseph Eisele.

The Bornoff Approach

George Bornoff developed a successful approach to teaching strings that focused for the left hand on the utilization of five finger patterns. When students became proficient in these five patterns, they were capable of performing music in any key at an early age or early stage of playing. Bornoff proposed that the entire fingerboard be learned as early as possible, so that two fingered scales and other left-hand exercises were employed early in a students instruction.

At the same time, the student developed right-hand technique through a variety of bowing studies that employed many fundamental bowing techniques almost from the beginning. These studies included up-bow and down-bow staccatos, spiccato, and détaché at varying bow speeds and utilizing the various segments of the bow. The function of these exercises was to build a tonal base that would result in a beautiful sound.

The initial books were all technical studies but later, songbooks were published to accompany the technical études. These "songbooks" utilized all finger patterns in a variety of keys. In addition, they used the various bow techniques learned so that the student could bring all of the right-and left-hand techniques into use in a musical setting.

Traditional Approaches

Probably the most successful of all traditional books are the ones that were developed from string-class teaching by Sam Applebaum. The complete series of Applebaum books cover every aspect of string playing. They follow all of the established pedagogical procedures and contain popular folk songs as well as early, easy string pieces. The series is published by Belwin/Mills.

Action with Strings by Robert Klotman, published by Southern Music Company, can best be described as an eclectic approach. It utilizes the finger patterns and bowing studies that one finds in the Bornoff books but is built around musical pieces that follow a sequence based on skill and technical development. The basic levels follow traditional patterns and students acquire vocabulary and cognitive knowledge about music as they progress through the book.

Appendix

Special Projects and Assignments

1.   There have been several successful approaches to class string instruction. Each one has its unique features and has proved successful in a variety of situations. A competent string teacher should be well informed as to the various approaches and method books that are available, as well as their advantages and disadvantages. It would be a good idea, as a class assignment, to make comparative studies of some of the methods currently on the market. There are many more in addition to those listed below, but these are a few that have special impact on the philosophy of string teaching today.

Appelbaum, Sam: *String Builder*, Belwin-Mills
Gerald E. Anderson and Robert S. Frost: *All for Strings*, Kjos
Bornoff, George: *Finger Patterns*, Thompson (Carl Fischer, selling agent)
Farish, Margaret, and Owens, Don: *Shapes and Sounds*, Presser
Green, Elizabeth: *Hohmann for the String Class*, Carl Fischer
Herfurth, Paul: *Tune a Day*, Boston Music
Isaac, Merle: *String Method*, Cole
Klotman, Robert: *Action with Strings*, Southern
Matesky, Ralph, and Womack, Adele: *Learn to Play a String Instrument*, Alfred Music
Müller, J. Frederick, and Rusch, Harold: *String Method*, Kjos
Rolland, Paul (revised by Sheila Johnson): *Young Strings In Action*, Boosey & Hawkes
Suzuki, Shinichi (Kendall, John—adaptation): *Listen and Play*, ZEN-ON, Summy-Birchard
Wisniewski, Thomas, Higgins, George, *Learning Unlimited String Program*, Leonard

2.   Review periodicals

American Suzuki Journal (published by the Suzuki Association of the Americas, P.O. Box 354, Muscatine, Iowa 52761)
The American String Teacher (published by the American String Teachers Association, P.O. Box 49-0039, Key Biscayne, Florida 33149)
The Instrumentalist (200 Northfield Road, Northfield, Illinois 60093)
The Music Educators Journal (published by the Music Educators National Conference, 1201 Sixteenth Street, N.W., Washington, D.C. 20036)

Graded Materials List and Literature

The American String Teachers Association periodically publishes lists that are useful for the classroom teacher. The following lists are available from Theodore Presser Co., Bryn Mawr, Pa. 19010

A Short List of Unusual Solo String Literature Arranged to Accommodate School Orchestras by Robert H. Klotman. (Secured from the School of Music, Indiana Univ., Bloomington, In. 47405)

String Syllabus: Organization of Auditions. Graded List of Studies, Scales, and Pieces for Violin, Cello, and Bass.

Using Orchestral Excerpts as Study Materials (A progressively graded survey; performance problems of each excerpt noted) by James Smith.

Suggested Materials for String Orchestra

A list of materials is obsolete the moment it is prepared. In addition, it is not feasible to select materials from a list or review without examining them. The following is only a suggested list to help teachers become acquainted with available sources, and is by no means comprehensive. It is merely a guide to enable teachers to initiate programs.

Key

E   = Easy
M   = Medium
D   = Difficult
MP = Multiple parts, enabling performance from "easy" to "difficult"

M	Adler: *Concertino for String Orchestra*, G. Schirmer
ME	Adler: *Four Early American Tunes*, G. Schirmer
ME	Anderson: *Suite of Carols*, Belwin-Mills
M	Anderson: *Jazz Pizzicato*, Belwin-Mills
M	Anderson: *Plink, Plank, Plunk!* Belwin-Mills
D	Bach: *Concerto in C Minor*, Breitkopf and Hartel (AMP) (Two Pianos)
MD	Bach: *Pastoral Symphony from "Christmas Oratorio,"* Oxford University Press
ME	Bach-Carse: *Air & Bourée* (from Suite No. 3 in D) Galaxy
M	Bach-Carse: *Rondeau* (from Suite No. 3 in D), Galaxy
MD	Bach-Issac: *Brandenburg Concerto No. 3*, Etling
E	Bartok-Applebaum: *Moods*, Belwin-Mills
ME	Bartók-Weiner: *Ten Pieces*, Boosey & Hawkes
MD	Bartók-Willner: *Roumanian Folk Dances*, Boosey & Hawkes
ME	Berger: *Boulderollicks*, Summy-Birchard
MD	Berger: *Hayride*, Summy-Birchard
M	Berger: *Short Overture*, G. Schirmer
M	Biber: *Battalia*, Kerby
M	Bohm-Applebaum: *Sarabande*, Belwin-Mills
MD	Britten: *Simple Symphony*, Oxford University Press
E	Carse: *Two Little Dances*, Galaxy
E	Clark (Editor): *Introduction to String Quartets*, Boston Music
M	Corelli: *Christmas Concerto*, Oxford University Press and Sam Fox Music
M	Corelli: *Concerto Grosso, Op. 6, No. 3*, Broude
M	Dancla-Klotman: *Herald Quartet* Belwin-Mills
M	Delius: *Air and Dance*, Boosey & Hawkes
ME	Dello Joio: *Air for Strings*, Edward B. Marks Music
ME	Diemer: *Pavane*, Carl Fischer
E	DiLasso-Klotman: *Echo Fantasy*, FEMA

ME   Farish: *Concerto Grosso*, Cole
M   Fletcher: *Folk Tune and Fiddle Dance*, Boosey & Hawkes
ME   Frackenpohl: *Suite for Strings* (based on American folk songs), G. Schirmer
ME   Frost: *My Favorite Ice Cream Is Chocolate*, Kendor Music
ME   Gardner: *Country Moods*, G. Schirmer
M   Gates: *Varicolor Variations*, Boosey & Hawkes
D   Gordon: *Three Preludes*, Bourne
ME   Green: *Theme and Variations* (Étude for Orchestra Bowing), Carl Fischer
M   Grieg: *Suite, "From Holberg's Time"*, Kalmus
M   Handel: *Overture* (Stoessel University String Orchestra Album), Carl Fischer
E   Handel-Siennicki: *Little Fugue*, Etling
M   Handel-Sontag: *Finale from the "Water Music"*, Sam Fox Music
MD   Haydn-Klotman: *Midnight Minuet*, Alfred
ME   Haydn-Woodhouse: *Serenade* (from *String Quartet, Op. 3, No. 5*), Boosey & Hawkes
D   Hindemith: *Eight Pieces*, Schott-American Music
E   Holesovsky: *Variations on a French Folk Tune*, Elkan Music
D   Holst: *St. Paul's Suite*, G. Schirmer, Curwen
MD   Hovhaness: *Psalm and Fugue*, Skidmore Music
M   Hovhaness: *Psalm & Fugue*, C. F. Peters
ME   Hunt: *English Airs for String Orchestra*, Carl Fischer
E   Isaac: *Marionettes*, Carl Fischer
ME   Johnson: *Cremona String Ensemble Folio*, Carl Fischer
D   Kay: *Six Dances*, Music Corporation of America/Leeds
M   Kirk: *Hemis Dance*, Carl Fischer
M   Kreutzer-Chassman: *Salute to Kreutzer*, G. Schirmer
E   Kuhn: *Twenty-Five 16th and 17th Century Dance Tunes and Airs*, Carl Fischer
E   Lichner-Applebaum: *Gypsy Dance*, Belwin-Mills
M   Lutoslawski: *Five Folk Melodies*, D.M.W./Leonard
E   MacDowell-Applebaum: *To a Wild Rose*, Belwin-Mills
E   McKay: *Accent on Strings* (vol. 1–2), Music Publishers Holding Corporation
ME   McKay: *Music of the Americas*, Summy-Birchard
ME   McKay: *Port Royal*, Summy-Birchard
M   Mozart: *Six Country Dances*, Breitkopf & Hartel, Associated Music
MD   Mozart: *Serenade, "A Little Night Music"* (Stoessel University String Orchestra Album), Carl Fischer
Me   Nelhybel: *Triptych for Strings*, Colin Music
ME   Pachelbel-May: *Canon*, Schott
E-M-D *Polychordia Library*, Galaxy
M   Purcell: *Overture to "The Rival Sisters,"* Belwin-Mills
M   Purcell: *Suite from "Abdelazer,"* Novello (Gray)
ME   Purcell-Britten: *Chacony*, Boosey & Hawkes
M   Purcell-Klotman: *Sonata in F*, Belwin-Mills
ME   Purcell-Stoessel: *Suite from "Dido and Aeneas,"* G. Schirmer
M   Purcell-Whittaker: *Chaconne in G Minor*, Oxford University Press
ME   Satie-Klotman: *Gymnopedie*, Edward B. Marks Music
ME   Scheidt-Klotman: *Suite for Strings*, Alfred

ME	Shapiro (Arranger): *Chanukah Music for Strings*, Etling
ME	Siennicki: *Scherzo for String Orchestra*, Kjos
E	Siennicki: *Country Dance*, Kjos
E	Steg: *Five Arrangements for Strings* (Handel, Mozart, Rossini, Weber, Brahms), Summy-Birchard
MP	Steg: *Concertino Piccolo*, Skidmore Music
ME	Strauss-Isaac: *Rosenkavalier Waltzes*, Boosey & Hawkes
D	Tchaikovsky: *Serenade, Op. 48*, Associated Music
M	Torelli: *Christmas Concerto*, Kahnt, Associated Music
MP	Vaughan-Williams: *Concerto Grosso*, Oxford University Press
ME	Vitali: *Concerto in D Minor* (Two Solo Violins), Sam Fox Music
M	Vivaldi-Kird: *Air and Country Dance* (from "The Seasons"), Sam Fox Music
MD	Warlock: *Capriol Suite*, Curwen (G. Schirmer)
M	Washburn: *Serenade for Strings*, Oxford University Press
ME	Whear: *Petite Suite for Strings*, Ludwig Music
ME	Whitney: *Dance Suite for Strings*, Warner Brothers Music
ME	Withers: *Fete Galante*, Belwin-Mills

Solo Music for the Violin

Easy

Biehl-Applebaum: *Hobgoblin Dance*, Belwin-Mills
Bornoff: *Fun for Fiddle Fingers*, Thompson
Carse: *The Violin Teacher*, Boston Music
Fletcher: *Cornstalk Tunes*, Boston Music
Fletcher: *Fiddle Dance*, Boosey & Hawkes
Gardner: *Journey Through the Forest*, G. Schirmer
Gibb: *In Melody Land*, Broadcast Music
Mele: *First Adventures with the Violin*, Theodore Presser
Suzuki (Editor): *Suzuki Violin School*, bks. 1 and 2, Birch Tree Group
Tansman: *Seven French Pieces*, Associated Music

Medium-Easy

Benjamin: *Tune and Variations for Little People*, G. Schirmer
Beyer-Applebaum: *Dance of the Clowns*, Belwin-Mills
Cazden: *Four Favors, op. 87*, Shawnee
Kroll: *Contra-Dance*, G. Schirmer
Kroll: *Donkey Doodle*, G. Schirmer
Lichner-Applebaum: *Gypsy Dance*, Belwin-Mills
Moffat: *Old Masters for Young Players*, Associated Music
Moskowski-Applebaum: *Spanish Dance*, Belwin-Mills
Mozart-Applebaum: *A Viennese Sonatina*, Belwin-Mills
Perlman: *Indian Concertino*, Carl Fisher
Reiding: *Concertino, Op. 36, D Major*, Belwin-Mills

Medium

Bakaleinkoff: *Gavotte*, Belwin-Mills
Bartók: *Hungarian Folk Songs*, From "For Children," EMB
Beethoven: *Country Dances*, Oxford University Press
Dyer: *In the Row*, Belwin-Mills

Dyer: *Tempo Di Gavotta*, Belwin-Mills
Green: *Playful Rondo*, Willis Music
Handel: *Bourrée and Hornpipe*, Schott & Co.
Heiden: *Sonatina*, AMP
Huber-Klotman: *Concertino No. 4*, Carl Fischer
Kuchler: *Concertino, Op. 11*, Century Music
Lichner-Applebaum: *Gypsy Dance*, Belwin-Mills
Mendelssohn, L.-Klotman: *Student Concerto*, Carl Fischer (with orchestra accompaniment)
Ortiz: *Dulce Memoire*, Music Corporation of America
Prokofieff-Forst: *Kije's Wedding*, Edition Musicus
Ravel-Maganini: *Pavane*, Edition Musicus
Rolland-Fletcher: *First Perpetual Motion*, Belwin-Mills
Schubert-Applebaum: *Marche Militaire*, Belwin-Mills
Seitz-Klotman: *Concerto No. 4*, Belwin-Mills

Third Position

Bohm: *Sarabande in G Minor*, Carl Fischer
Fletcher: *New Tunes for Strings, Vol. 2*, Boosey & Hawkes
Handel: *Gavotte*, Elkan Music
Huber: *Concerto No. 2*, Carl Fischer
Prokofieff-Lipemann: *Three Pieces from "Music for Children,"* G. Schirmer
Rieding: *Concertino 1, Op. 21*, Belwin-Mills
Schubert: *Three Sonatines*, Associated Music
Seitz: *Concerto No. 2*, Carl Fischer
Setiz-Klotman: *Student Concerto*, First Movement from No. 5 in D Major (available with orchestra accompaniment), Belwin-Mills
Ten Have: *Allegro Brillante*, G. Schirmer

Additional Repertoire for Building Musicianship

Accolay: *Concerto in A Minor*, Southern Music (with orchestra accompaniment); Carl Fischer
Applebaum: *20 Progressive Solos for String Instruments*, Belwin-Mills
Corelli: *Sonatas*, Associated Music
Dancla: *Six Airs Varies* (Book I), G. Schirmer
Francoeur-Kreisler: *Siciliano et Rigaudon*, Charles Foley
Granado-Kreisler: *Spanish Dance*, Charles Foley
Klotman-Burkhalter: *String Literature for Expanding Technique*, FEMA
Kriesler: *Liebeslied*, Charles Foley
Kuchler: *Concerto in C Major, Op. 15*, Belwin-Mills
MacDowell-Hartmann: *To a Wild Rose*, Schmidt (Summy-Birchard)
Murray and Tate: *More Tunes for My Violin*, Boosey & Hawkes
Pracht: *Twelve Easy Pieces*, Boston Music
Suzuki: *Suzuki Violin School*, Vols. 1–5, Summy-Birchard
Vivaldi: *Concerto in A Minor*, Associated Music

Solo Music for the Viola

There are literally hundreds of excellent solos of all grades of difficulty. Except for those of artist grade, sonatas and concerti of intermediate grade for students are not so plentiful and are largely transcriptions. Nearly all the violin études are available for viola, transcribed. Many viola parts adapted to string-class methods may be used for individual teaching. The following lists are arranged in order of difficulty.

Solos with Piano Accompaniment

First Position

Aletter: *Melodie*, Carl Fischer
Bach-Johnstone: *Three Pieces*, Belwin-Mills
Bay (Editor): *Fun with the Viola*, Mel Bay
Beriot-Applebaum: *Serenade*, Belwin-Mills
Dunhill: *The Willow Brook*, Belwin-Mills
Dyer: *Old Redcoat*, Belwin-Mills
Dyer: *On the Serpentine*, Belwin-Mills
Gossec: *Gavotte*, Carl Fischer
Hauser: *Berceuse*, Carl Fischer
Müller: *Andante Contabile*, Kjos
Rowley: *Farandole*, Belwin-Mills
Rowley: *Scherzo*, Belwin-Mills
Seitz-Klotman: *Concerto No. 5*, Belwin-Mills (with orchestra accompaniment)
Siennicki: *Highland Heather*, Kjos

Third Position

Album of Classical Pieces, vols. I, II, III, International Music
Bach-Forbes: *Jesu, Joy of Man's Desiring*, Oxford University Press
Brunson: *Bariolage Badinage*, Kjos
Docktor: *Solos for the Viola Player*, G. Schirmer
Forbes (Editor): *Chester Music for Viola*, Chester Music
Gurlitt: *Scherzino*, Schmidt
Harvey: *The Viola Players Repertory*, Ditson
Heacox: *Ten Easy Solos*, Ditson
Maganini: *Concert Album for Viola and Piano*, Edition Musicus
Ponce: *Estrellita*, Carl Fischer
Tchaikowsky: *Chanson Triste*, Carl Fischer
Whistler-Hummel: *Concert and Contest Album*, Rubank

Collections with Piano Accompaniment

First Position

Forbes: *A First Year Classical Album*, Oxford University Press
Kritch: *First Book of Viola Pieces*, Witmark
Murray-Tate: *Tunes Old and New*, Oxford University Press
Stoutmaire and Henderson: *Duets for All*, Belwin-Mills
Suzuki: *Viola School, Vols. I–5*, Summy-Birchard Music
34 Viola Solos, Belwin-Mills
Whistler: *Solos for Strings* (viola), Rubank

Solo Music for the Cello

First Position and Extensions

Deak: *Autumn Song, and Lullaby*, Belwin-Mills
Dottlein, Ed.: *Collection of Small Pieces*, vol. I, Schott
Fletcher: *New Tunes for Strings*, vol. I, Boosey & Hawkes

Hollaender: *Six Easy Pieces*, Boston Music
Krane: *Classical and Folk Melodies*, Presser
Moffat: *Old Masters for Young Cellists*, Associated Music
Nash: *Prelude, Barcarolle, a Memory*, G. Schirmer
Nelson: *Right from the Start*, Boosey & Hawkes
Otis: *First Book of Study Pieces*, Boston Music
Popejoy: *The Singing Cello*, Belwin-Mills
Popejoy: *Melodious Studies for Cello*, Belwin-Mills
Squire: *In Dreamland*, Carl Fischer
Suzuki (Editor): *Suzuki Cello School*, vols. 1 and 2, Birch Tree Group
Whistler: *Solos for Strings*, Rubank
Rentmeister (Editor): *Easy Violincello Duets*, C. F. Peters

First and Fourth Positions and Extensions

Alexander: *Southward Bound Suite*, Associated Music
Corker: *In Ireland Suite*, Associated Music
Grant: *Duets for Two Cellos*, Ludwig Music
Gretchaninoff: *Early Morn Suite*, Associated Music
Herfurth: *Classical Album of Early Grade Pieces*, Boston Music
Jarnefelt: *Berceuse*, Carl Fischer
Krane: *Bach for the Cello*, G. Schirmer
Suzuki (Editor): *Suzuki Cello School*, vols. 3–5, Birch Tree Group
Tansman: *Nous jouons pour Maman*, Associated Music

First Four and Half Positions and Extensions

Breval: *Sonata in C Major*, Associated Music
Cellist's Solo Album, Carl Fischer
Cirri: *Arioso*, Edition Musicus
DiBiase: *Reverie*, Carl Fischer
Fletcher: *New Tunes for Strings*, vol. 2, Boosey & Hawkes
Martini: *Gavotte*, G. Schirmer
Mendelssohn: *Student Concerto in D*, Carl Fischer (with orchestra accompaniment)
Romberg: *Sonata in B Flat, Op. 43, No. 1*, International Music
Schroeder, *Easy Violoncello Classics*, Book I, Boston Music
Squire: *Danse Rustique*, Carl Fischer
Ticciati: *12 Concert Pieces*, Oxford University Press
Webster: *Scherzo*, Boston Music

Additional Solos for the Cello

For additional solo material for the cello player, see Louis A. Potter, Jr.'s *Graded List of Materials and Repertoire for Cello*. Extended lists may also be found in the appendix of *The Art of Cello Playing* by Louis A. Potter, Jr. (published by Summy-Birchard).

Solo Music for the String Bass

Easy

Bakalanova: *Ten Easy Pieces*, Leeds Music
Bakaleinikoff: *Valse*, Belwin-Mills
Bratton-MacLean: *Teddy Bear's Picnic*, Music Publishers Holding Corporation

Carrol: *Five Simple Pieces for the Double Bass*, Augener
De Coursey, Ralph: *Six Easy Pieces*, BMI-Canada
Drew: *First Sonatina*, Belwin-Mills
Isaac: *Jolly Dutchman*, Carl Fischer
Isaac: *Nautical Medley, The Jolly Dutchman*, Carl Fischer
Lesinsky: *Thirty-Four String Bass Solos*, Belwin-Mills
Merle: *Mummers*, Carl Fischer
Schemuller: *Prayer*, Carl Fischer
Schuman-Applebaum: *The Strange Man*, Belwin-Mills
Siennicki: *Highland Heather*, Kjos
Whistler: *Solos for Strings*, Rubank

Medium

Anderson, A. C.: *Sonatina*, Carl Fischer
Bach-Zimmerman: *Gavotte*, Carl Fischer
Bakaleinikoff: *Allegro Moderato*, Belwin-Mills
Cirri: *Arioso*, Edition Musicus
Corelli-Zimmerman: *Sarabande*, Carl Fischer
Drew: *Second Sonatina*, Belwin-Mills
Gates, Everett: *Night Song*, Boosey & Hawkes
Gossec-Skalmer: *Gavotte*, Volkwein
Handel-Thompson: *Allegro for String Bass*, Carl Fischer
Handel-Zimmerman: *Largo*, Jenkins Music
Kohler: *Two Austrian Folk Tunes*, Belwin-Mills
Lesinsky (Arranger): *34 String Bass Solos*, Belwin-Mills
Merle: *Caballero*, Carl Fischer
Purcell: *Aria*, International Music
Vivaldi-Zimmerman: *Intermezzo* (from Concerto in D Minor), G. Schirmer
Walter, David: *The Elephant's Gavotte*, Yorke Edition

Medium-Difficult

Capuzzi: *Concerto*, Boosey & Hawkes
Pergolesi-Zimmerman: *The Giorni*, Carl Fischer
Marcello: *Sonata in E Minor*, International Music
Marcello: *Sonata in F Major*, International Music
Marie-Sevitzky: *La Cinquantine*, G. Ricordi
Ostrander: *Album for String Bass and Piano*, Edition Musicus
Zimmerman: *Bach for the Young Bass Player*, MCA Music

Additional Literature for the String Bass

An extended list and analysis of easy to more advanced repertoire is available in the *Comprehensive Catalogue of Literature for the String Bass* by Murray Grodner, published at Indiana University.

Portnoi, Henry: *Creative Bass Technique*, Logan, American String Teachers Association (Presser), 1978), 110 p.

Films and Filmstrips

Key

AFI   Artists Films, Inc., 366 Madison Ave., New York, New York
BF   Brandon Films, 200 West 57th Street, New York, New York

BOW	Stanley Bowmar Co., 12 Cleveland St., Valhalla, New York
BYU	Brigham Young University, Department of Audio-Visual Communication, Provo, Utah
CFD	Classroom Film Distributors, Inc., 5620 Hollywood Blvd., Los Angeles, California
CORF	Coronet Films, Coronet Bldg., Chicago, Illinois
DISNEY	Walt Disney Productions, Educational Film Division, 350 South Vista Ave., Burbank, California
EBF	Encyclopedia Britannica Films, 1150 Wilmette Ave., Wilmette, Illinois
FA	Film Association of California, 11559 Santa Monica Blvd., Los Angeles, California
FACSEA	French-American Cultural Services and Educational Aid, Audio Visual Dept., 972 Fifth Ave., New York, New York
HOFFBERG	Hoffberg Productions, Inc., 321 W. 44th St., New York, New York
IU	Indiana University, Audio-Visual Center, Bloomington, Indiana
JH	Jam Handy, Detroit, Michigan
LES	Irving Lesser Enterprises, 527 Madison Ave., New York, New York
LOCKMA	Lockheed MSD Management Association, Audio-Visual Productions, Department 81–72, Bldg., 181–N, Sunnyvale, California
MGHT	McGraw-Hill Textfilms, 330 West 42nd St., New York, New York
NFBC	National Film Board of Canada, 680 Fifth Ave., New York, New York
SF	Sterling Educational Films, 241 E. 34th St., New York, New York
S&R	Scherl and Roth, Inc., C. G. Conn, Elkhart, Indiana
UMTV	University of Michigan TV, 310 Maynard St., Ann Arbor, Michigan
UN	University of Nebraska, Bureau of Audio-Visual Instruction, Extension Division, Lincoln, Nebraska
UW	University of Wisconsin, Bureau of Audio-Visual Instruction, 1312 West Johnson St., Madison, Wisconsin

Films

LES	Arthur Rubinstein, Jascha Heifetz and Gregor Piatigorsky (Mendelssohn Trio in D Minor)
UMTV	Baroque Cello Recital
CFD	Basic Violin Playing—Tone Production and Vibrato
LOCKMA	California Youth Symphony Orchestra
EBF	Casals Conducts
UMTV	Cellist and His Music
FA	Cello, Part I
FA	Cello, Part II
SF	Cello Concert
EBF	Children's Concert, Part III (String Instruments)
LES	Coolidge Quartet

BF	Country Fiddle No. 1
BF	David Oistrakh Playing "Mazurka" by Zarzycki
BF	David Oistrakh Playing "Slavonic Dance in E Minor" by Dvorak-Kreisler
LES	Dimitri Mitropoulos and the New York Philharmonic Orchestra
SF	Eine Kleine Nachtmusik
LES	Emanuel Feuermann
SF	Emperor Waltz
BF	Fantasy for Four Strings
LES	Gregor Piatigorsky
UMTV	Haydn and Mozart
LES	Hollywood String Quartet, The
CORF	Instruments of the Orchestra—The Strings
LES	Jascha Heifetz—Portrait of an Artist
EBF	Listening to Good Music—The String Quartet
HOFFBERG	Malaguena
IU	Meaning of Chamber Music
FACSEA	Metamorphoses Du Violoncello, Les
UMTV	Music of the Quintet
CFD	Musical Instruments—The Strings
UW	Musical Performance Improvement for the Violin (Two Parts)
LES	New York Philharmonic Orchestra
LES	Pablo Casals in Prado (Bach Suite No. 1)
EBF	Pablo Casals, A Legend Come to Life
IU	Pablo Casals—Master Class at Berkeley, 4, Beethoven Sonata No. 3 in A Major, Op. 69
AFI	Paganini Caprices
EBF	Playing Good Music
IU	Sonata, The
IU	Sound of a Stradivarious
UMTV	Sound of Strings
NFBC	Story of a Violin
BYU	Story of Chamber Music
EBF	String Choir, The (2nd ed.)
IU	String Quartet and Its Music, The
CORF	String Trio, The
EBF	Suzuki Teaches American Children and Their Mothers
EBF	Symphony Orchestra, The (2nd ed.)
SF	Tchaikovsky Concert (Leonard Rose)
DISNEY	Toot, Whistle, Plunk and Boom
NFBC	Toronto Symphony No. 1
NFBC	Toronto Symphony No. 2
LES	Trio, The-Rubinstein, Heifetz and Piatigorsky
FA	Violin, The (Part I)
BF	Violinist, The
IU	Voices of the String Quartet
MGHT	What is a Concerto? (Leonard Bernstein)
MGHT	What is a Melody? (Leonard Bernstein)

Filmstrips

S&R	Art of Bow Making, The
UN	Instrumental Instructional Filmstrips (Strings)
JH	Instruments of the Symphony Orchestra (String)
BOW	Meet the Instruments of the Symphony Orchestra
EBF	String Instrument Care
S&R	Violin Making in Europe and Violin Adjusting in the USA

Recommended Reading

APPLEBAUM, Samuel, and APPLEBAUM, Sada, *With the Artists* (series). Neptune, N.J. Paganiaiana Publications, 1958–1985

AUER, Leopold, *Violin Playing.* Philadelphia: Lippincott, 1960

BOYDEN, David, *The History of Violin Playing from its Origins to 1761.* London: Oxford University Press

COOK, Clifford A., *String Teaching and Some Related Topics.* Bryn Mawr: Presser, American String Teachers Association, 1957

DOLEJSI, Robert, *Modern Viola Technique.* Chicago: University of Chicago Press, 1939. (Reprinted by ASTA 1960), 133 p.

EPPERSON, Gordon, *The Art of Cello Teaching.* Bryn Mawr: Presser, American String Teachers Association, 1980, 58 p.

FARGA, Franz, *Violins and Violinists.* London: Camelot, 1955, 223 p.

FLESCH, Carl, *The Art of Violin Playing: Technique in General, Applied Technique.* Book I. New York: Fischer, 1939. 171 p.

FLESCH, Carl, *The Art of Violin Playing: Artistic Realization and Instruction.* Book II. New York: Fischer, 1930. 231 p.

GALAMIAN-GREEN, *Principles of Violin Playing and Teaching.* Englewood Cliffs: Prentice-Hall, 1962, 108 p.

GEMINIANI, Francesco, *The Art of Playing on the Violin* (1751). Edited by David D. Boyden. New York: Oxford University Press. 51 p. (Reprint)

GRODNER, Murray, *Comprehensive Catalogue of Literature for the String Bass.* Bloomington: Indiana University, 1958, 58 p.

HAVAS, Kato and LANDSMAN, Jerome *Freedom To Play.* New York: ABI/Alexander Broude, 1981, 115 p.

HODGSON, Percival, *Motion Study and Violin Bowing.* Presser, American String Teachers Assoc., 1983, 106 p. (Reprint)

JACKSON, BERMAN, and SARCH, *The A. S. T. A. Dictionary of Bowing Terms.* Byrn Mawr: Presser, American String Teachers Association, 1987, 73 p.

JALOVEC, Karel, *Beautiful Italian Violins.* New York: Tudor, 1964, 111 p.

KRALL, Emil, *The Art of Tone Production on the Violin and Cello.* London: Oxford University Press, 1923, 87 p. (May be secured through Oscar Shapiro, 2901 18th Street, N.W., Washington, D.C.)

KRASNER, Louis, ed., *Tanglewood String Symposium.* Stockbridge: Berkshire Music Center, 1965, 98 p.

KROLICK, Edward, *Basic Principles of Double-Bass Playing.* Washington, D.C.: Music Educators National Conference, 1959, 14 p.

MILLS and SUZUKI: Parents, *In the Suzuki Style*. Diablo Press, 1974, 119 p.

MOZART, Leopold, *Violin Playing*. London: Oxford University Press, 1959. (Reprint) 225 p.

NORAYN, Deane, *The Small Stradivari* (a novel). New York: Abelard-Schuman, 1961. 223 p.

POLNAUER and MARKS, *Senso-Motor Study and Its Application to Violin Playing*. Urbana: American String Teachers Association, 1966. 266 p.

POTTER Jr., Louis, *The Art of Cello Playing*. Princeton: Summy-Birchard, 1964, 227 p.

PRIMROSE, William, *Technique Is Memory*. New York: Oxford University Press, 1960.

RABIN, Marvin, and SMITH, Priscilla, *Guide To Orchestral Bowings Through Musical Styles* (a manual to be used with video). Madison: University of Wisconsin Extension Arts, 1984, 64 p.

READ, Gardner, *Thesaurus of Orchestral Devices*. London: Pitman, 1953, 631 p.

RETFORD, William C., *Bows and Bow Makers*. London: The Strad, 1964, 86 p.

ROLLAND, Paul, *Basic Principles of Violin Playing*. Washington, D. C.: Music Educators National Conference, 1959, 54 p.

ROSENBERG, Fred, *The Violin, The Technic of Relaxation and Power*. Bryn Mawr: Presser, American String Teacher Association, 1987, 27 p.

SCULLY, F. E., *A Scientific Approach to Better Intonation*. Hollywood: Scully, 1958, 10 p.

SILVERMAN, William, *The Violin Hunter* (a novel). New York: Day, 1957, 256 p.

SKOLBERG, Phyllis, *The Strings: A Comparative View*. Bloomington: Frangipani, 1982, 218 p.

STANTON, David, *The String Double Bass*. Evanston: "The Instrumentalist," 1965, 72 p.

SZIGETI, Joseph, *Szigeti on the Violin*, London: Vassell, 1969, 227 pp.

SZIGETI, Joseph, *With Strings Attached*. New York: Knopf, 1961, 330 p.

WASSEL and WERTMAN, *Bibliography for String Teachers*. Washington, D. C.: Music Educators National Conference, rev. 1964, 40 p.

YOUNG, Phyllis, *Playing the String Game*. Austin: University of Texas Press, 1978, 97 p.

Selected readings from "The Strad," published by J. H. Lavender and Co., 2 Duncan Terrace, London, N. I.

Published lists and bulletins by The Music Educators National Conference and the American String Teachers Association.

String Instrument Inspection Record

The care-and-maintenance list that follows was prepared by Dr. Paul Van Bodegraven, formerly chairman of the Department of Music, New York University, and was first published by the Educational Division of Scherl & Roth, Inc. It is a valuable aid to potential string teachers in determining whether instruments are in the best possible playing condition. It has been expanded by this author. All answers should be "yes."

		YES	NO
A. PEGS			
1.	Do they fit snugly in both peg-hole openings?	☐	☐
2.	Do they turn smoothly and silently?	☐	☐
3.	Do they hold in position with slight inward pressure while turning?	☐	☐
B. FINGERBOARD NUT			
1.	Do all strings clear the fingerboard without buzzing when playing open or stopped strings?	☐	☐
2.	Are the string grooves in the fingerboard nut shallow?	☐	☐
C. FINGERBOARD			
1.	Is it smooth with no grooves?	☐	☐
2.	Is it glued securely onto the neck?	☐	☐
3.	Is it free of excess glue along edges?	☐	☐
4.	Is it the proper height?	☐	☐
5.	Has it been wiped clean?	☐	☐
D. BRIDGE			
1.	Is it the proper height?	☐	☐
2.	Do the feet fit perfectly with the top contour?	☐	☐
3.	Is the E string on the low side of bridge (violin) A string on viola and cello, G string on bass?	☐	☐
4.	Is it set opposite the inside notches on the F holes?	☐	☐
5.	Are all string grooves shallow?	☐	☐
6.	Is it perfectly straight, not warped?	☐	☐
7.	Does it lean slightly towards the tailpiece?	☐	☐
8.	Is there sufficient arch so the student does not have difficulty playing from one string to the other?	☐	☐
E. TAILPIECE			
1.	Is the small end of tailpiece almost even with the outside edge of saddle?	☐	☐
2.	Is there some space between it and top of instrument?	☐	☐
3.	Is there a clearance between tailpiece and chinrest?	☐	☐
F. STRINGS			
1.	Are all perfectly smooth, without kinks?	☐	☐
2.	Is the metal winding tight?	☐	☐
3.	Are the adjusters on all metal strings working smoothly?	☐	☐
4.	Are the strings free of caked rosin?	☐	☐
5.	Do you have an extra set of strings in your case?	☐	☐
6.	Are your reserve strings sealed from dryness?	☐	☐
7.	If you have any steel strings on your instrument, are they equipped with adjusters?	☐	☐
8.	Have you checked to be sure that the strings are not false?	☐	☐
9.	Are the strings wound straight on all pegs?		

	YES	NO
G. INSTRUMENT BODY		
1. Is it free from open cracks?	☐	☐
2. Is the top clean and free of caked rosin?	☐	☐
3. Are the front and back thoroughly glued to the ribs?	☐	☐
H. THE SOUNDPOST		
1. Is it directly behind the right foot of the bridge?	☐	☐
2. Is it perpendicular to top and back?	☐	☐
3. Is the soundpost setter slot facing the right F hole?	☐	☐
I. THE BOW		
1. Can it be loosened and tightened freely?	☐	☐
2. Does it have enough hair?	☐	☐
3. Does the hair extend the full width of the frog ferrule?	☐	☐
4. Has it been rehaired in the past year?	☐	☐
5. Is the bow stick free of caked rosin?	☐	☐
6. Does it have real wire winding and leather thumb grip?	☐	☐
7. Is the bow arch noticeable and not warped when it is tightened ready to play?	☐	☐
8. Is there a protective facing, ivory or metal, on the tip?	☐	☐
9. Is the frog free from cracks?	☐	☐
J. CHINREST		
1. Is the chinrest securely attached to instrument?	☐	☐
2. Is the chinrest free of broken edges?	☐	☐
3. Is it of proper height for correct posture and comfortable playing?	☐	☐
K. ROSIN		
1. Do you have a full size (unbroken) cake of rosin?	☐	☐
2. Do you have a clean cake of rosin?	☐	☐
3. Are you using rosin for the individual bow, that is, (violin, cello, bass rosin)?	☐	☐
L. MUTE		
1. Do you have a mute available ready for instant use?	☐	☐
M. CELLO AND BASSES		
1. Is the adjustable endpin in proper working order?	☐	☐
2. Do you have a cello or bass endpin rest that prevents instrument slipping while playing?	☐	☐
K. CASES		
1. Do the locks close tightly?	☐	☐
2. Is the handle secure?	☐	☐

Repairing String Instruments

Repairing a string instrument requires a skilled, knowledgeable repairman. Maintenance, however, can be done by any concerned, responsible individual who is willing to take the time to acquire information regarding a few simple procedures. In addition there are some minor repairs that a teacher can do to help the student through a critical moment.

It is important, however, that teachers realize that there are limitations to what they can repair even under emergency situations. When such a situation occurs, they should leave these repairs to a reputable repairman. Too often serious damage has been done to string instruments by uninformed, well-intentioned, amateur repair persons.

Proper Adjustment

It is important that string instruments be in good working condition (properly adjusted) for the following reasons:

1. Proper adjustment provides for a better sound.
2. When the instrument is out of adjustment, students become frustrated by the handicaps created. Proper adjustment facilitates playing.
3. When playing is made easier and sounds better, it increases the student's pride and confidence in performing ability.

Minor Repairs

When a string breaks, follow these procedures:

1. Loop it through the hole in the tail piece or hook it to the tuner.
2. Place the opposite end through the opening in the appropriate peg and wind the string so the winding moves toward the wall of the peg box and does *not* cross another string.
3. If a metal string is being used, be certain that the bridge pad (protector) is in the groove to prevent the string from cutting into the bridge.

Replacing a bridge requires a great deal of skill and knowledge. Following are a few rules that might be helpful in an emergency:

1. *Never* glue the feet of the bridge to the top of the violin.
2. Try and find a bridge that matches the height of the broken bridge. It is imperative that the bridge not be too high or too low. (When the bridge is assembled, test it by feeling; try playing a few notes.)
3. To have the feet fit the top properly, put a piece of fine sandpaper on the top, under the place where the feet of the bridge will go, *with the abrasive side up* facing the bridge. Then gently rub the feet on the sandpaper at the appropriate spot so that the paper sands the feet until they fit the top of the violin snugly. Match the grooves with the broken bridge before cutting the notches. When assembling the bridge with the violin and strings, be certain that the *high* side is under the G string. Tilt the bridge slightly back toward the tailpiece so that the pressure from the strings is focused on the center of the bridge.

A warped bridge must be replaced. However, a temporary solution is to soak it in water over night. Allow it to dry *standing* so that it will get air from all sides.

If the bridge is too low, it can be raised by placing a small piece of cardboard under each foot. If it is too high, remove some wood from the top edge and then make new grooves. "Also, make sure the string notches are only 1/3 of the string thickness deep."[1]

Miscellaneous parts that can be handled easily:

1. If tailgut breaks, keep a supply of Sacconi tailguts on hand. They can be screwed on and adjusted to length easily and quickly.
2. Stock tuners for emergency replacements.
3. Keep a chin rest key on hand at all times to tighten chin rests when they become loose and fall off.
4. If using Caspari pegs, keep a key handy to tighten screw in pegs.

In an emergency some corrections can be made to secure proper bow-hair tension.

1. If the hair is too long, put some cardboard under the hair at the tip so that it will increase the tension. This is only a temporary solution.
2. If the hair is too short, wet the hair and pull two equally divided parts of hair around the stick and to the back. Brace the hair and hold it in place with a small object like a toothpick. Be certain to wrap something like string around the tip to make it secure and prevent it from breaking.
3. If the eyelet thread becomes stripped, pinch it with pliers just enough to make the screw work.
4. When the button comes off, melt some rosin and put in the hole. Then insert the screw.
5. Wash dirty hair in very soapy water with a toothbrush and hang it to dry.

Major Repairs

These should be done entirely by a professional repairman

1. Cracks in the body of the instrument are caused by stress. Find the source.
2. Gluing the fingerboard or adjusting the height and curvature by planing should not be done by the uninitiated.
3. Bow rehairing needs a professional hand.
4. Adjusting the sound post requires a sound-post adjuster and expert knowledge regarding placement and its affect on tone.

Factors Affecting an Instrument's Tone

1. A bow that needs rehairing results in a glassy, sliding sound.
2. Improper adjustment and not having the sound post in its most productive position can cause difficulties in playing as well as affect tone. These factors will vary from instrument to instrument.
3. The quality of the instrument is important. This does not mean that a student needs the best instrument, but it does imply that there is a point of diminishing return when purchases are based entirely on cost.

---

[1] Horn, Peter, *Emergency Repair Manual.* Cleveland: Horn and Son Stringed Instruments, 2570 Superior Avenue, Cleveland, Ohio 44114.

There should be a minimum standard in terms of tone and construction that one will accept. A poor-sounding instrument will discourage a student and result in economic loss in terms of teaching time expended on a losing cause.

Measurements and Terminology of Sizes[1]

I. Instrument Terminology for Measurements

A. The body length is measured from the top shoulder (upper edge where the neck joins the body) to the end of the lower bout (base of the instrument).

B. The string length is measured from the edge of the nut (where fingerboard meets nut) to the bridge. Actually, it is the open-string length that vibrates when played.

1. Violin and Viola: The body distance (diapason) between the inside notch of the F-hole (on the soundpost side) to the upper edge of the top (where the neck joins the body) should represent three-fifths of the string length.

2. Cello: The diapason should represent ten-seventeenths of the string length.

3. Bass: The diapason should represent four-sevenths of the string length.

II. Instrument Measurements

Violin	Size	Body Length Inches	Body Length cm	String Length Inches	String Length cm
Standard (full)	4/4	14	35.56	12 7/8	32.70
Intermediate	3/4	13 1/4	33.66	12	30.50
Junior	1/2	12 7/16	31.59	11 5/16	28.73
Bantam	1/4	11	27.94	10 1/64	26.44
Bantam	1/8	10	25.40	9 5/32	23.26
Bantam	1/10	9 1/4	23.50	8 9/32	21.03
Bantam	1/16	8 1/2	21.59	7 25/64	18.80

Bantam sizes vary, depending upon the country of manufacture.

Viola	Size	Body Length Inches	Body Length cm	String Length Inches	String Length cm
Standard (full)	Large	16 1/2 and up	41.90 and up	15	38.1
Standard (full)		16	40.64	15	38.1
Standard (full)		15 1/2	39.40	14 11/64	36.0
Standard (full)	Small	15	38.1	13 31/32	35.5
Intermediate		14	35.56	12 7/8	32.70
Junior		13 1/4	33.66	12	30.50

Cello	Size	Body Length Inches	Body Length cm	String Length Inches	String Length cm
Standard (full)	4/4	29 5/8	75.25	27 1/2	69.9
Intermediate	3/4	27 5/16	69.40	24 3/4	62.87
Junior	1/2	25 1/2	64.77	23 1/4	59.05
Bantam	1/4	22 3/4	57.79	20 3/4	52.71
Bantam	1/8	20 1/8	51.12	18 18/32	47.15

[1] Prepared by Edward C. Campbell, Luthier, The Chimneys Violin Shop, for the MENC Ad Hoc Committee on minimum standards.

Bass	Size	Body Length		String Length	
		Inches	cm	Inches	cm
Standard	3/4	43 1/4 to	109.86 to	41 1/2 to	105.40 to
Standard	3/4	44 1/2	113.0	43 5/16	110.0
Intermediate	1/2	38 5/8 to	98.11 to	38 3/4	98.43
Intermediate	1/2	41 1/4	104.78	38 3/4	98.43
Junior	1/4	35	88.9	—	—
Bantam	1/8	—	—	—	—

III. BOWS
   A. The bow length is measured from the tip to the end of the screw
      button. Bows should be proportionate to the size of the instrument
      used.

Violin Bow	Size	Length	
		Inches	cm
Standard	4/4	29 1/4	74.30
Intermediate	3/4	27	68.58
Junior	1/2	24 1/2	62.23
Bantam	1/4	22 1/8	56.20
Bantam	1/8	19 1/4	48.90
Bantam	1/10*	19 1/4	48.90
Bantam	1/16*	16 3/16	42.70

*Both use same size fiberglass bow, 1/16 size

Viola Bow	Size	Length	
		Inches	cm
Standard	4/4*	29 1/4	74.30
Intermediate	3/4*	29 1/4	74.30
Junior	1/2*	27	68.60

*Intermediate (14") violas use the same length bow as a 4/4 violin, but the 14" and up viola should use a
viola bow under all circumstances. Smaller violas may use violin bows.

Cello Bow	Size	Length	
		Inches	cm
Standard	4/4	28 1/8	71.40
Intermediate	3/4	26 7/16	67.15
Junior	1/2	25 1/2	64.77
Bantam	1/4	23 1/2	59.69
Bantam	1/8	20 5/8	52.39
Bantam	1/10	17 1/2	44.45

Bass Bow	Size	Length	
		Inches	cm
Standard	French 3/4	28 3/4	73.03
Standard	German 3/4	30 3/8	77.15
Intermediate	French 1/2	26 1/2	67.30
Intermediate	German 1/2	27 3/4	70.49
Junior	1/4 - use half-size bows.		

French or German (Butler) bass bows are acceptable in all sizes

   B. Bow Materials
      1. Pernambuco wood—first choice for better quality instruments
      2. Brazilwood
      3. Fiberglass—acceptable for 1/16 and 1/8 size instruments

C. Bow Hair Materials
  1. Natural horse hair—unbleached hair
  2. Synthetic hair—must be texturized
  3. White hair is preferred for advanced (solo) students, however, mixed hair is quite acceptable.
  4. Bow hair should be "sighted down" to make sure there are no crossed or twisted hairs.

Fingering Charts

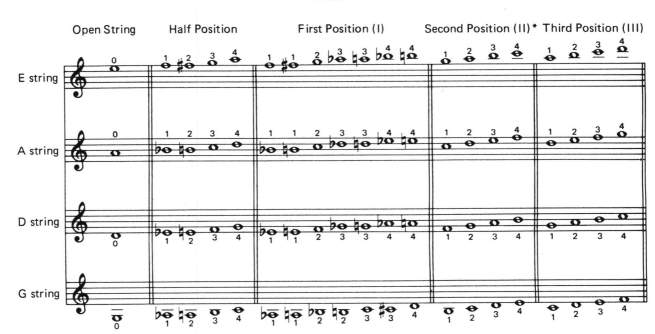

Violin

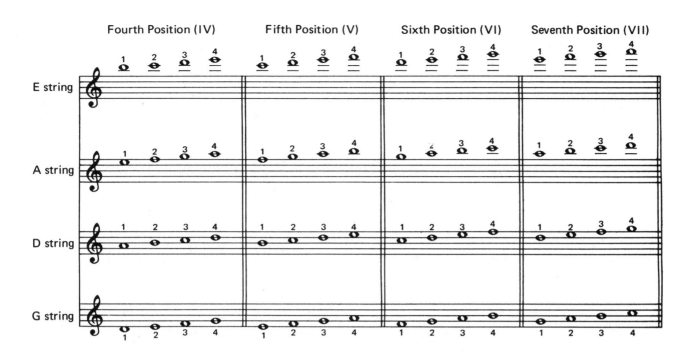

*Beginning with the second position, accidentals are omitted so that the chart can be followed more easily. A rule to follow in the beginning is that accidentals generally use the same finger, raised or lowered, as the uninflected note. Examples:

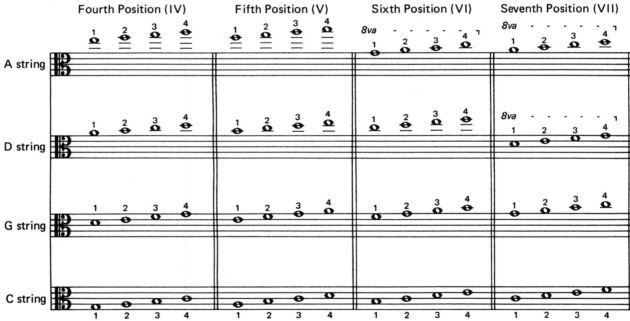

*Beginning with the second position, accidentals are omitted so that the chart can be followed more easily. A rule to follow in the beginning is that accidentals generally use the same finger, raised or lowered, as the uninflected note. Examples:

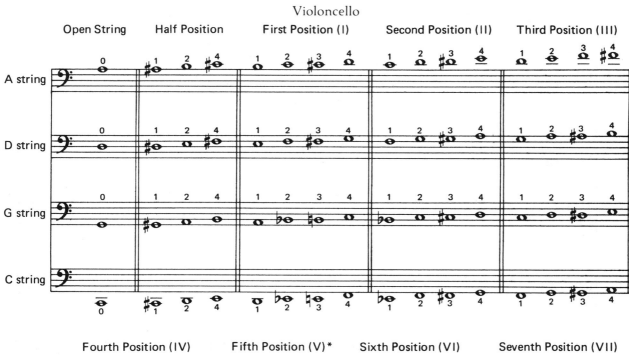

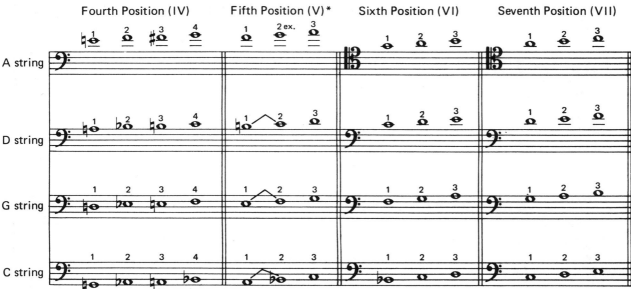

*Beginning with the fifth position, not all of the accidentals are included. The chart is merely a guide; the intervals determine the correct relationships in finger placement.

Thumb Position

At the seventh position the cellist has reached the point of maximum reach for the hand. He then employs the thumb position. The thumb is placed where the first finger was located in seventh position, one octave above the open string (see figure). The sign for the use of the thumb is ♀. The thumb position uses both the tenor and treble clefs. The following is the fingering for the D major scale in thumb position:

D string

String Bass

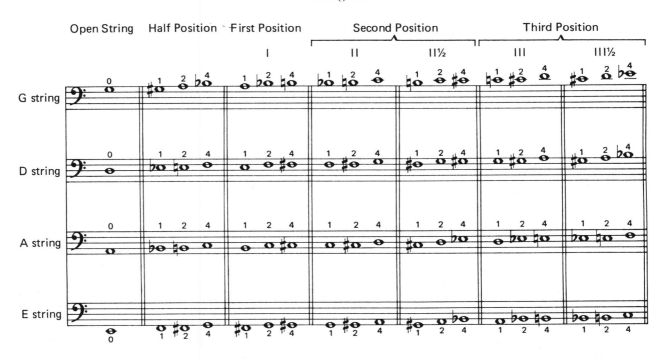

Glossary for Strings

The American String Teachers Association has published a comprehensive *Dictionary of Bowing and Pizzicato Terms* by Barbara Seagrave, Joel Berman, and Kenneth Sarch. It may be secured from Theodore Presser Company.

A due corde (It.), Upon two strings **Allonger l'archet** (Fr.), Lengthen the bow stroke

A punta d'arco (It.), At the point of the bow

Arco (It.), Use the bow

Arpeggio (It.), Notes of a chord played in broken fashion

A una corda (It.), On one string

Bogen (Ger.), Violin bow

Coll'arco (It.), Play with the bow

Collé, A bowing in which the string is pinched lightly, followed by a lift to prepare for the next stroke (see p. 176)

Col legno (It.), With the wood part of the bow (see p. 173)

Con sordini (It.), With mutes

Corda (It.), String

Cordatura (It.), The notes to which the strings, any strings, are tuned

Coup d'archet (Fr.), Stroke of the bow

Détaché (Fr.), Literally "detached"—any form of separated bowing on the string (see p. 162)

Down-bow, Sign is ⊓; the bow is drawn from the hand away from the instrument

Double stop, Playing simultaneously on two strings (see p. 91)

Due corde (It.), Two strings

Flautando (It.), Light, airy; played over the fingerboard

Frog, The lower end of the bow, to which the hair is fastened

Glissando (It.), Slide the fingers in gliding manner

Head, Point of the violin bow

Legato (It.), Smooth or sometimes tied together (⌒).

Leggiero (It.), Light, delicate

Legno (It.), Wood or stick part of the bow (see p. 173)

Lever l'archet (Fr.), Lift the bow

Louré (Fr.), Bowing style for pulsed or legato notes (see p. 171)

Marcato (It.), Refers to an accentuated or well-marked style of bowing

Martelé (Fr.), Hammered or sharply accented style of bowing (see p. 167)

Mute, A small clamp made of various metals or wood and placed on the bridge to dampen the sound of the instrument

Neck, That part of a string instrument extending from the head to the body; the fingerboard is attached to it

Nut, The small bridge at the upper end of the fingerboard over which the strings pass into the peg box; sometimes it is used synonymously with the frog

Parlando (It.), In a declamatory style, using a variety of expressive bowings as if "to speak"

Piqué (Fr.), A martelé style of bowing at the tip

Pointe (Fr.), Tip of the bow

Ponticello (It.), Bow close to the bridge to produce a "squeaky" effect (see p. 172)

Portamento (It.), Gliding effect from note to note for expressive purposes

Punta (It.), The point or bow tip

Ricochet (Fr.), A bouncing style of bowing that involves two or more slurred notes; the bow is dropped on the string so that it ricochets

Saltando (It.), Leaping, skipping the bow

Sautillé (Fr.), A rapid bouncing bow that occurs through the natural resiliency of the stick

Scordatura (It.), A special tuning of the open strings (see p. 177)

Spiccato (It.), A bouncing bow that is controlled by the hand (see p. 168)

Staccato (It.), Detached and distinctly separated bowling (see p. 164)

Sul tasto (It.), Over the fingerboard (see p. 174)

Tip, Head of the bow

Tremolo (It.), A note or chord reiterated at a rapid rate; it may or may not be measured (see p. 169)

Una corda (It.), On one string only

Up-bow, The sign is V; start at the point of the bow and move the hand toward the instrument

Index